CHOCOLATE CHIP

Paleo Chocolate Cookbook for Guilt-free Desserts

(Delicious and Easy Chocolate Truffle Recipes That Everyone)

Cory Guardado

Published by Alex Howard

© **Cory Guardado**

All Rights Reserved

Chocolate Chip: Paleo Chocolate Cookbook for Guilt-free Desserts (Delicious and Easy Chocolate Truffle Recipes That Everyone)

ISBN 978-1-990169-25-0

All rights reserved. No part of this guide may be reproduced in any form without permission in writing from the publisher except in the case of brief quotations embodied in critical articles or reviews.

Legal & Disclaimer

The information contained in this book is not designed to replace or take the place of any form of medicine or professional medical advice. The information in this book has been provided for educational and entertainment purposes only.

The information contained in this book has been compiled from sources deemed reliable, and it is accurate to the best of the Author's knowledge; however, the Author cannot guarantee its accuracy and validity and cannot be held liable for any errors or omissions. Changes are periodically made to this book. You must consult your doctor or get professional medical advice before using any of the suggested remedies, techniques, or information in this book.

Table of contents

PART 1 1

INTRODUCTION 2

Chocolate Or Devil Food Cake 3
Chocolate Ice Cream 5
Dark Chocolate Mousse 6
Chocolate Cupcakes 7
German Chocolate Cake 9
Chocolate Marble Cake 12
Chocolate Lovers Cheesecake 13
Chocolate Chip Cookies 14
Chocolate Molasses Kisses 15
Chocolate Popcorn Balls 16

FUDGE CHOCOLATE RECIPES 17

Fudgy Chocolate Brownies 17
Pistachio Fudge 18
Caramel Topped Vanilla Bean Fudge 19
Sweet Lime Fudge 20
S'mores Fudge 21
Oreo Cookie Fudge 22
Birthday Cake Fudge 24
Easy Nutella Walnut Fudge 25
Vanilla Bundt Cake With Fudge 26
Pumpkin Pecan Chocolate Fudge 28
Milk Chocolate Fudge 30
Red Velvet Fudge 31
White Chocolate Cranberry Fudge 32
Butter Pecan Fudge 33
Cappuccino Fudge 35
Cinnamon Sugar Fudge 36
Cherry Fudge With Dark Chocolate 38
Rocky Road Fudge 39
Chocolate Raspberry Truffle Fudge 40

COCONUT CHOCOLATE FUDGE WITH ALMONDS	41
CANDY CANE FUDGE	43
SPICY MEXICAN CHOCOLATE FUDGE	44
BUTTERSCOTCH FUDGE	45
CLASSIC HOT FUDGE SAUCE	46
CHOCOLATE PRETZEL FUDGE	47
CHOCOLATE POMEGRANATE FUDGE	48
PEANUT BUTTER FUDGE	49
BROWN SUGAR FUDGE	50
POPCORN FUDGE	51

HOT CHOCOLATE RECEPIES 52

CREAMY HOT COCOA	52

HOT COCOA POWDER MIX 53

CREAMY HOT CHOCOLATE	54
EASY MEXICAN HOT CHOCOLATE	55
CANDY CANE COCOA	56
MICROWAVE HOT CHOCOLATE	57
TRIPLE RUSH HOT CHOCOLATE	58
VEGAN HOT CHOCOLATE	59
ITALIAN HOT CHOCOLATE	60
PEANUT BUTTERCUP HOT CHOCOLATE	61
SPICED HOT CHOCOLATE	62
MAYAN HOT CHOCOLATE	63
HOMESTYLE HOT COCOA	64
CREAMY VEGAN HOT COCOA	65
WHIPPED HOT CHOCOLATE	66
THIN MINT COCOA	67
CHOCOLATE BAR HOT CHOCOLATE	68
PUMPKIN SPICE HOT CHOCOLATE	69
KOCOA KLASTCH BLEND	70
CHOCOLATE LOVER'S HOT CHOCOLATE	71
MEXICAN-STYLE HOT CHOCOLATE	72
CHAMPURRADO	73
COCONUT HOT COCOA	74

HAWAIIAN HOT CHOCOLATE	75
FROZEN HOT CHOCOLATE	76
SMOOTH HOT CHOCOLATE	77
ORANGE HOT CHOCOLATE	77
DARK CHOCOLATE HOT COCOA	79
CINNAMON HOT CHOCOLATE MIX	80
NUTELLA HOT CHOCOLATE	81
ULTRA-RICH HOT CHOCOLATE	82
CARAMEL HOT CHOCOLATE	83
NEW ENGLAND HOT CHOCOLATE	84
MOSCOW HOT CHOCOLATE	85
BRAZILIAN HOT CHOCOLATE	86
BELGIAN HOT CHOCOLATE	87
SPANISH HOT CHOCOLATE	88
FRENCH STYLE HOT CHOCOLATE	89
HOT SPICED NEW ENGLAND CIDER	90
HAZELNUT HOT CHOCOLATE	91
PART 2	**92**
CHOCOLATE TRUFFLE CHEESECAKE	93
CHOCOLATE TRUFFLE RASPBERRY CHEESECAKE	95
CHOCOLATE TURTLE CHEESECAKE	98
CHOCOLATE-CARAMEL TOPPED CHEESECAKE	100
CHOCOLATE-CHERRY CHEESECAKE BARS	102
CHOCOLATE-COVERED CHEESECAKE SQUARES	104
CHOCOLATE-COVERED WHITE CHEESECAKE	107
CHOCOLATE-GLAZED COCONUT ALMOND CHEESECAKE	109
CHOCOLATE-MARBLED CHEESECAKE DESSERT	112
CHOCOLATE-TOPPED CHOCOLATE CHEESECAKE	114
CHOCOLATE-TOPPED STRAWBERRY CHEESECAKE	117
CHOCOLATY ALMOND CHEESECAKE	120
COCONUT-WHITE CHOCOLATE CHEESECAKE	122
COFFEE LOVER'S MINI CHEESECAKES	124
CONTEST-WINNING WHITE CHOCOLATE CHEESECAKE	126
CRANBERRY MOCHA CHEESECAKE	129
CRANBERRY ORANGE CHEESECAKE	132

CRANBERRY WHITE CHOCOLATE CHUNK CHEESECAKE	135
DELUXE CHIP CHEESECAKE	137
DOUBLE CHIP CHEESECAKE BARS	140
DOUBLE CHOCOLATE ALMOND CHEESECAKE	142
DOUBLE CHOCOLATE ESPRESSO CHEESECAKE	145
DRESSED-UP CHEESECAKE	148
DULCE DE LECHE CHEESECAKE	149
EASY CHEESECAKE PIE	151
EASY CHOCOLATE CHERRY CHEESECUPS	153
FABULOUS FUDGE CHEESECAKE	155
FAVORITE LEMON CHEESECAKE	157
FESTIVE HOLIDAY CHEESECAKE	159
FESTIVE WHITE CHOCOLATE CHEESECAKE	161
FROSTED CHOCOLATE CHIP CHEESECAKE	164
FROSTY SUMMER DESSERT	166
FROZEN BROWNIE CHEESECAKE	168
FROZEN CHEESECAKE BITES	170
FROZEN CHOCOLATE CHEESECAKE TART	172
FROZEN MOCHA CHEESECAKE	174
FROZEN MOCHA CHEESECAKE LOAF	176
FROZEN MOCHA CHEESECAKES	178
FROZEN MOCHA TORTE	180
FROZEN RASPBERRY CHEESECAKE	182
FUDGE TRUFFLE CHEESECAKE	184
GERMAN CHOCOLATE CAKE CHEESECAKE	186
GERMAN CHOCOLATE CHEESECAKE SQUARES	189

Part 1

Introduction

For years we've heard eating chocolate is not good for you. But there is good news for dark chocolate lovers. On top of being delicious, dark chocolate is rich in fiber, iron, magnesium, copper, manganese, and other minerals that are good for your health.

Dark chocolate has the ingredient cocoa bean, that is rich in flavants, and antioxidants that prevents damage to the cells and organs. It can help to avoid against heart disease, keep cholesterol from accumulating in the blood level and improve blood flow. It also improves the function of the brain. The cocoa act as stimulants like caffeine and theobromine, which can enhance brain function in no time.

With 70 percent cocoa, dark chocolate can also be used as a skin regiment. It contains bio active that is great for the skin. The flavonoids protect against sun damage, improve blood flow to the skin and increases skin density, hydration, complexion, and it also absorbs UV light.

Though dark chocolate is good for you, it should be eaten in small portions to get the antioxidants, while limiting the amount of calorie intake but take note that calories and fat can differ between brands.

I enjoy chocolate whether it is light or dark and I want to share some of my favorites recipes

Chocolate Or Devil Food Cake

Cooking spray
1 cup unsweetened cocoa powder
2 1/2 cups all-purpose flour
2 cups sugar
1 1/2 teaspoons baking powder
1 teaspoon baking soda
1 teaspoon salt
3 large eggs, at room temperature
3/4 cup vegetable oil
1/2 cup sour cream
2 teaspoons vanilla extract

Directions

1. Preheat the oven to 350 degrees F. Coat two 9-inch-round cake pans with cooking spray and line the bottoms with parchment paper.
2. Whisk the cocoa powder and 1 1/2 cups boiling water in a medium bowl until smooth; set aside. Whisk the flour, sugar, baking powder, baking soda and salt in a large bowl until combined. Add the eggs, vegetable oil, sour cream and vanilla and beat with a mixer on medium speed until smooth, about 1 minute. Reduce the mixer speed to low; beat in the cocoa mixture in a steady stream until just combined, then finish mixing with a rubber spatula.
3. Divide the batter between the prepared pans and tap the pans against the counter to help the batter settle. Bake until a toothpick inserted into the middle comes out clean, 30 to 40 minutes. Transfer to racks

and let cool 10 minutes, then run a knife around the edge of the pans and turn the cakes out onto the racks to cool completely. Remove the parchment. Trim the tops of the cakes with a long serrated knife to make them level, if desired.

Chocolate Ice Cream

8 large egg yolks
1 cup sugar
1/4 teaspoon coarse salt
2 cups skim milk
1/2 cup unsweetened cocoa powder
2 cups heavy cream

Directions

1. In a medium saucepan, off heat, whisk together egg yolks, sugar, and salt until blended. Stir cocoa powder into egg-yolk mixture. Gradually whisk in milk.

2. Cook over medium, constantly stirring with a wooden spoon until custard thickens slightly and evenly coats back of spoon (it should hold a line drawn by your finger), 10 to 12 minutes.

3. Pour custard through a fine-mesh sieve into a bowl set over ice. Stir in cream. Let stand, occasionally stirring, until chilled. Churn in an ice cream maker according to manufacturer's instructions. Transfer ice cream to a resealable plastic container and freeze until firm, about 2 hours (or up to 3 months).

Dark Chocolate Mousse

5 1/4 ounces bittersweet chocolate, coarsely chopped
14 ounces cold heavy cream
3 large egg whites
1 -ounce sugar
Sweetened whipped cream, for garnish, optional
Shaved bittersweet chocolate, for garnish, optional
Directions

1.Place chocolate in a large bowl set over a bainmarie or in a double boiler at a low simmer. Stir chocolate until melted. Turn off the heat and let stand.

2. Beat the cream over ice until it forms soft peaks. Set aside and hold at room temperature. With a mixer, whip egg to soft peaks. Gradually add the sugar and continue whipping until firm.

3. Remove the chocolate from the bainmarie and using a whisk, fold in the egg whites all at once. When the whites are almost completely incorporated, fold in the whipped cream. Cover the mousse and refrigerate for approximately 1 hour or until set. Serve in goblets topped with more whipped cream and shaved chocolate, if desired.

Chocolate Cupcakes

3/4 cup unsweetened cocoa powder
3/4 cup all-purpose flour
1/2 teaspoon baking powder
1/4 teaspoon salt
3/4 cup (1 1/2 sticks) unsalted butter, room temperature
1 cup sugar
3 large eggs
1 teaspoon vanilla extract
1/2 cup sour cream
White Icing
Directions

1. Preheat oven to 350 degrees. Line 12-cup standard muffin tin with paper liners.
2. Into a medium bowl, sift together cocoa, flour, baking powder, and salt; set aside. In a mixing bowl, cream butter and sugar until light and fluffy. Add eggs, one at a time, beating well after each, then beat in vanilla. With mixer on low speed, add flour mixture in two batches, alternating with sour cream and beginning and ending with flour.
3. Pour batter into cups, filling each 3/4 full. Bake until a toothpick inserted in centers comes out clean, 20 to 25 minutes.
4. Cool in pan 5 minutes; transfer to a wire rack to cool completely, then spread with Easy White Icing using a table knife or small offset spatula. Decorate with sprinkles, if desired.

German Chocolate Cake

1 cup vegetable oil, plus more for greasing the pans
2 1/2 cups all-purpose flour, spooned and leveled, plus more for dusting the pans
1/4 cup unsweetened cocoa powder
1 teaspoon baking soda
1/2 teaspoon fine salt
4 ounces semisweet chocolate, roughly chopped
2 cups granulated sugar
3 large eggs, at room temperature
1 cup milk

Filling:
1 1/2 cups pecans
1 cup milk
3 large egg yolks
3/4 cup packed light brown sugar
4 tablespoons unsalted butter
1/4 cup corn syrup
1 teaspoon vanilla extract
1/4 teaspoon fine salt
1 1/2 cups sweetened shredded coconut

Frosting:
8 ounces semisweet chocolate, chopped
1 cup plus 2 tablespoons heavy cream

Special equipment: a pastry bag fitted with a star tip
Directions

For the cake: Preheat the oven to 350 degrees F. Lightly coat two 9-inch round cake pans with oil and dust with flour. Whisk together the flour, cocoa, baking soda and salt in a small bowl; set aside.

Microwave the chocolate in a small microwave-safe bowl on high power for 45 seconds; remove and stir. Microwave again at high power in 30-second increments, stirring in between, until the chocolate has melted completely; set aside.

Beat the granulated sugar, oil and eggs in a large bowl with an electric mixer on medium speed until smooth. Beat in the melted chocolate. Alternate beating in the flour mixture and the milk, adding the flour in three additions and the milk in two, starting and ending with the flour until just incorporated. Add half the milk, and mix until just combined. Repeat with the remaining flour mixture and milk, making sure not to overmix. Divide the batter evenly between the prepared pans.

Bake until a toothpick inserted in the center comes out with moist crumbs, 30 to 35 minutes. Let cool in the pans for 10 minutes, run a thin spatula around the edges and then turn the cakes out onto a cooling rack to cool completely. (They will have a sugary "crust" on the top. This is from the melted chocolate and is not a problem. It will soften once the cake is assembled or if the layers are baked the day before.)

For the filling: While the cakes cool, spread the pecans on a baking sheet and bake, tossing once, until toasted, 8 to 10 minutes. Finely chop. Whisk together the milk and egg yolks in a medium saucepan until smooth. Add the brown sugar, butter, corn syrup, vanilla and salt, and cook over medium heat, constantly stirring, until the mixture has thickened and coats the back of a spoon, 5 to 6 minutes. Pour the mixture into a large bowl. Stir in the coconut and pecans; set aside to cool.

For the frosting: Put the chocolate in a medium bowl. Heat 1 cup of the cream in a small saucepan over medium heat until steaming but not boiling, and pour over the chocolate. Let stand a few minutes, and then whisk until smooth; let stand at room temperature (or put in the refrigerator if your kitchen is hot) until thick but not set, 20 minutes to 1 hour. Add the remaining 2 tablespoons cream to the chocolate mixture, and beat with an electric mixer on medium speed until lightened in color and fluffy, about 1 minute. The frosting should hold medium peaks and will continue to firm up a bit as it stands. Spoon about 1 cup frosting into a pastry bag fitted with a star tip.

To assemble: Put one cake layer right-side up on a serving plate, and top with half the filling. Top with the second cake layer and the remaining filling, spreading it to about 1/2 inch from the edge. Frost the sides, and decorate around the top edge of the cake with the frosting in the pastry bag.

Loosely cover the cake with plastic wrap and leave at room temperature overnight. Unwrap and serve.

Chocolate Marble Cake

2 cups all-purpose flour
2 teaspoons baking powder
1/2 teaspoon salt
1 cup white sugar
1/2 cup butter, softened
2 eggs
1 teaspoon vanilla extract
1 cup milk
2 tablespoons unsweetened cocoa powder
Directions

1.Preheatoven to 350 degrees F (175 degrees C). Grease and flour a 9 inch round pan.

2.Place flour, baking powder, salt, sugar, butter or margarine, eggs, vanilla, and milk into mixing bowl. Beat slowly to moisten, then beat with an electric mixer at medium speed for about 2 minutes until smooth. Reserve 3/4 cup batter; pour the remainder into pan.

3.Stir cocoa into the 3/4 cup reserved batter. Drop by spoonfuls over top of white batter. Using a knife, swirl the cocoa batter into the white batter to incorporate it in a marble effect.

4.Bake in preheated oven for 30 to 35 minutes, until an inserted wooden pick, comes out clean.

Chocolate Lovers Cheesecake

4 (1 ounce) squares semisweet chocolate, chopped
2 (8 ounce) packages cream cheese, softened
1/2 cup white sugar
1/2 teaspoon vanilla extract
2 eggs
1 (9 inch) prepared chocolate cookie crumb crust
Directions

1. Preheat oven to 350 degrees F (175 degrees C.) In the top of a double boiler, heat chocolate, occasionally stirring, until chocolate is melted and smooth. Remove from heat and allow to cool to lukewarm.

2. In a large bowl, beat the cream cheese, sugar, and vanilla until smooth. Slowly beat in eggs, one at a time. Blend in melted chocolate. Pour filling into crust.

3. Bake in the preheated oven for 40 minutes, or until filling is set. Allow to cool. Refrigerate for at least 3 hours before serving.

Chocolate Chip Cookies

1 cup butter, softened
1 cup white sugar
1 cup packed brown sugar
2 eggs
2 teaspoons vanilla extract
3 cups all-purpose flour
1 teaspoon baking soda
2 teaspoons hot water
1/2 teaspoon salt
2 cups semisweet chocolate chips
1 cup chopped walnuts
Directions

1. Preheat oven to 350 degrees F (175 degrees C).
2. Cream together the butter, white sugar, and brown sugar until smooth. Beat in the eggs one at a time, then stir in the vanilla. Dissolve baking soda in hot water. Add to batter along with salt. Stir in flour, chocolate chips, and nuts. Drop by large spoonfuls onto ungreased pans.
3. Bake for about 10 minutes in the preheated oven, or until edges are nicely browned.

Chocolate Molasses Kisses

2 cups of coffee
1/3 a cup of glucose (pure corn syrup)
2/3 cups of water
1 cup of molasses
2 teaspoons of butter
1/4 tablespoon of salt
4 ounces of Chocolate
1 tablespoon of vanilla extract (or 1 teaspoonful of essence of peppermint)

Directions

Put all the ingredients, save the salt, chocolate, and flavoring, over the fire; let boil rapidly to 260F or until brittle when tested in cold water. During the last of the cooking, the candy must constantly be stirred. Pour onto an oiled platter or marble; pour the chocolate, melted over hot water, above the candy; as the candy cools on the edges, with a spatula or the fingers, turn the edges towards the center; continue this until the candy is cold enough to pull; pull over a hook until cold; add the flavoring, a little at a time, during the pulling, cut in short lengths and wrap in waxed paper

Chocolate Popcorn Balls

1 1/2 cups of sugar
1/3 a cup of glucose
2/3 a cup of water
1/3 a cup of molasses
3 tablespoons of butter
2 tablespoons cocoa powder
1 teaspoon of vanilla extract
About 4 quarts of popped corn (well salted)
Directions

Set the sugar, glucose and water over the fire, stir until the sugar is melted, then wash down the sides of the saucepan, cover and let boil three or four minutes, then remove the lid and let cook without stirring to the hard ball degree; add the molasses and butter and stir continuously until brittle in cold water; remove from the fire and, as soon as the bubbling ceases, add the chocolate, melted over hot water, and the vanilla; stir, to mix the chocolate evenly through the candy, then pour onto the popped corn, mixing the two together meanwhile. With buttered hands lightly roll the mixture into small balls. Press the mixture together only just enough to hold it in shape. Discard all the hard kernels in the corn. Have the corn warm and in a warm bowl.

Fudge Chocolate Recipes

Fudgy Chocolate Brownies

Ingredients

- 1 cup sugar
- 6 tablespoons cocoa powder
- 1/2 teaspoon salt
- 2 teaspoons vanilla extract
- 1 large egg
- 2/3 cup all-purpose flour
- 1/2 teaspoon baking powder
- 3 tablespoons water
- 1/4 cup vegetable oil

Instructions

1. Preheat oven to 350 degrees and lightly grease an 8" x 8" pan. Set aside.

2. Combine all ingredients into a bowl and stir until mixed.

3. Pour the batter into lightly greased pan and bake for about 20 minutes.

4. Let cool and cut into squares to serve.

Pistachio Fudge

Ingredients

- 1/2 cup of shelled, unsalted pistachios
- 10 tablespoons unsalted butter
- 6 ounces dark chocolate
- 4½ cups sugar
- 7 ounces sweetened condensed milk
- Pinch of salt

Instructions

1. Line an 8" x 8" square baking pan with lightly greased parchment or wax paper. Set aside.

2. In a medium size saucepan, over low heat, combine all ingredients except pistachios and stir until the chocolate is melted and the mixture is creamy.

3. Once melted, add in the pistachios and stir until well-blended.

4. Pour and spread the fudge into the pan and let cool until the fudge has set. Cut into small squares and enjoy.

Caramel Topped Vanilla Bean Fudge

Ingredients

- 18 ounces white chocolate
- 14 ounces sweetened condensed milk
- 1/2 cup of caramel sauce
- 3 vanilla beans (seeds)
- 1 teaspoon vanilla extract

Instructions

1. Line an 8" x 8" pan with wax or parchment paper. Set aside.

2. In a medium sauce pan, over low heat, combine all of the ingredients, except the caramel sauce, vanilla bean seeds, and the vanilla extract. Stir until melted and remove from heat.

3. Scrape the seeds out of the vanilla beans and stir them into the mixture, as well as the vanilla extract.

4. Once well-blended, pour and spread about 1/3 of the fudge mix into the pan and then spread the caramel sauce over top.

5. Pour and spread the remaining fudge over caramel sauce.

6. Let the fudge chill in refrigerator until firm and set. Cut into squares and serve.

Sweet Lime Fudge

Ingredients

- 1 2/3 cups sugar
- 5-ounces 2% or whole evaporated milk
- 1/2 teaspoon salt
- 12 large marshmallows
- 2 cups white chocolate chips
- 1/4 cup grated lime zest
- 2 tablespoons key lime juice

Instructions

1. Line an 8" x 8" pan with lightly greased foil. Set aside.

2. In a large sauce pan, combine milk, sugar and salt and bring to a boil over medium heat. Boil for 8 minutes, while stirring.

3. Take the pan off of the heat and stir in marshmallows, chocolate, lime zest and lime juice. Mix until the marshmallows and chocolate are well melted and the mix is smooth.

4. Pour and spread the fudge into the pan and make sure the fudge covers the bottom evenly.

5. Let the fudge cool for 2 hours, then cut into 1-inch squares and enjoy!

S'mores Fudge

Ingredients

Graham Cracker
- 4 graham crackers
- 1 1/2 tablespoons melted butter
- 1/4 cup of sugar

Chocolate Fudge
- 1 1/2 cups milk chocolate chips
- 1/2 can of sweetened condensed milk
- 1/2 teaspoon vanilla extract

Marshmallow
- 1 cup white chocolate chips
- 1/2 can sweetened condensed milk
- 1/2 cup marshmallow fluff

Instructions

1. Preheat the oven to 375 degrees and line an 8" x 8" square pan with lightly greased foil. Set aside.

2. First, to make the graham cracker crust, crush the graham crackers up and mix in the melted butter and sugar. Pour and spread the graham cracker mixture into the pan and push down to make an even layer. Bake for 15 minutes and then set aside.

3. Next, to make the chocolate layer, heat the chocolate in small sauce pan over medium to low heat until it melts and then pour in half of the can of condensed milk and the vanilla. Once it is melted, pour it over the graham cracker crust.

4. Lastly, make the marshmallow layer; melt the white chocolate chips in a small sauce pan over medium-low

heat. Add in the marshmallow fluff and the rest of the sweetened condensed milk. Stir until it is melted and smooth and then pour over the chocolate layer.

5. Refrigerate overnight and then cut into small squares.

Oreo Cookie Fudge

Ingredients

- 15 oz of white chocolate
- 13-15 Oreos
- 8 oz of cream cheese, room temperature
- 4 cups powdered sugar
- 1 1/2 teaspoons vanilla extract

Instructions

1. Line an 8" x 8" pan with lightly greased parchment paper or wax paper. Set aside.

2. Mix cream cheese, powdered sugar, and vanilla into a large mixing bowl, and beat with a hand mixer until smooth and set aside.

3. Heat white chocolate in your double boiler until smooth. If you don't have a double boiler, set a glass bowl over a pot, filled with simmering water.

4. After the chocolate has melted, pour the chocolate and 3/4 of the Oreo cookies into the cream cheese

mixture and stir until combined. Pour the fudge mix into the pan and spread it evenly.

5. Sprinkle the remaining Oreo cookies into the fudge.

6. Let the fudge chill in the fridge for a few hours until firm. Remove from pan, cut into squares and serve.

Birthday Cake Fudge

Ingredients

- 2 ½ cups vanilla cake mix
- 3/4 cup white chocolate chips
- 2 cups powdered sugar
- 2/3 cups butter
- 1/2 cup sprinkles
- 1/4 cup milk

Instructions

1. Line a 9" x 9" pan with light greased parchment paper or wax paper. Set aside.

2. Combine vanilla cake mix and confectioners' sugar in a large mixing bowl. Without mixing in, add milk and butter into the bowl and heat in microwave for 2 minutes.

3. After carefully removing the bowl from the microwave, stir everything together immediately.

4. Fold in white chocolate until almost melted and add in the sprinkles. Stir gently.

5. Pour and spread the fudge mix into the pan and top with extra sprinkles.

6. Let the fudge cool in the refrigerator for a few hours until its cool. After its cool, cut into 2 inch squares and enjoy!

Easy Nutella Walnut Fudge

Ingredients

- 1 cup Nutella
- 1 teaspoon vanilla extract
- 2 sticks salted butter
- 1/4 teaspoon salt
- 4 cups powdered sugar
- 3/4 cup chopped walnuts

Instructions

1. Line an 8" x 8" pan with lightly greased foil. Set aside.

2. Combine the Nutella and butter in a microwave-safe bowl. Heat it in the microwave for 30 seconds at a time, stirring in between. After its melted, carefully remove the bowl from the microwave and add in the salt and vanilla. Stir until blended.

3. Make sure to sift the confectioners' sugar before adding it into the mixture. Fold in walnuts.

4. Pour and spread fudge evenly into the pan and refrigerate for a few hours until firm. After fudge is cool, cut into small pieces and serve.

Vanilla Bundt Cake With Fudge

Ingredients
Cake
- 1 cup butter
- 1 cup sugar
- 2 eggs
- 1 tablespoon vanilla
- 2 teaspoons baking powder
- 1/2 teaspoon salt
- 1/2 cup milk
- 1½ cups flour

Filling
- 5 ounces cream cheese
- 6 ounces melted, semi-sweet chocolate chips
- 1 egg

Instructions
1. Preheat oven to 325° and grease a Bundt pan with butter, dust with flour. Set aside.
2. In a large bowl combine and beat sugar and butter for 2 minutes until fluffy. You can use a hand mixer or standing mixer. Add in the eggs and vanilla and continue mixing until smooth. Stir in the baking powder and salt. Turn mixer to low and add in flour and milk. After mix is well-blended, set aside.
3. Add and beat the cream cheese in a different clean, mixing bowl until blended.
4. After you melt the chocolate chips, pour and stir them into the cream cheese, until it's smooth. Lastly,

beat in the egg into the mixture until it's completely mixed.

5. Pour and spread half of the cake batter into the bottom of the Bundt pan. Use a spoon to pour the chocolate filling into the center of the batter – make sure it stays in the center and doesn't touch the edges. Pour and spread the remainder of the cake batter on top of the chocolate.

6. Bake in the oven for 50- 55 minutes. Let the cake cool in the pan for 10 minutes and then invert pan onto a plate or platter. While the cake is still warm, whisk together 1 cup confectioners' sugar and 1 ½ tablespoons milk to make a glaze to drizzle onto the cake. Then the cake is ready to serve warm or cold.

Pumpkin Pecan Chocolate Fudge

Ingredients

Pumpkin

- 2 cups sugar
- 1 cup light brown sugar
- 5 ounces evaporated milk
- ¾ cup unsalted butter
- ½ cup pumpkin puree
- 3 teaspoons pumpkin pie spice
- 1 cup white chocolate chips
- 7 ounces marshmallow crème

Chocolate

- 2 cups sugar
- ¼ cup butter
- 5 ounces can evaporated milk
- 7 ounces marshmallow crème
- 1 tsp. vanilla extract
- 1 cup bittersweet chocolate chips
- 1 cup milk chocolate chips
- 1 cup chopped pecans

Instructions

1. Line a 9" x 9" pan with lightly greased wax paper. Set aside.

2. For the pumpkin, combine sugars, milk, butter, pumpkin puree and spice in a large sauce pan over medium heat. Stir until the mixture reaches a boil. Once boiling, stir constantly for about 10 minutes.

3. Remove pan from heat and add in white chocolate chips and marshmallow crème, stir until melted. Pour and spread pumpkin fudge into the pan and set aside.

4. For the chocolate, combine sugar, butter, evaporated milk and marshmallow crème in a pan over medium fire. Stir until the mixture reaches a boil. Once boiling, stir for 5 minutes.

5. Remove from heat and add in vanilla and chocolate chips, stir until melted. Pour chocolate over the pumpkin layer in the pan. Sprinkle pecans over top of chocolate.

6. Refrigerate for several hours until its cool. Once cool, remove fudge and cut into small squares and enjoy!

Milk Chocolate Fudge

Ingredients

- 3 cups milk chocolate or semi-sweet chocolate chips
- 14 ounces sweetened condensed milk
- 1/4 teaspoon salt
- 1 cup pecans (optional)
- 2 teaspoons vanilla

Instructions

1. Line an 8" x 8" pan with lightly greased foil. Set aside.

2. Combine chocolate chips, milk and salt in a medium saucepan, stir until melted.

3. Once the chocolate mixture is melted, remove pan from the heat and add in vanilla and nuts.

4. Pour and spread into pan. Let the fudge chill in refrigerator for a few hours. When it's cold and firm enough, cut into small squares and serve.

Red Velvet Fudge

Ingredients

- 3 cups of red velvet cake mix
- 2 cups of confectioners' sugar
- 10 tablespoons butter, cubed
- 5 tablespoons milk
- 3/4 cup white chocolate chips

Instructions

1. Lightly grease an 8" x 8" pan. Set aside.

2. In a large microwavable bowl, combine cake mix and powdered sugar. Add butter and milk and microwave on high for 2 minutes.

3. When finished, remove the bowl from the microwave and stir until mix is completely blended. Then stir in the chocolate chips until melted in.

4. Pour fudge into the pan and refrigerate for 2 hours or more. Once cool, cut into small squares and enjoy!

White Chocolate Cranberry Fudge

Ingredients
- 15 ounces white chocolate squares or chips
- 2 tablespoons unsalted butter
- 10 ounces sweetened condensed milk
- 3/4 cup of cranberry jam

Instructions
1. Line an 8" × 8" baking pan with lightly greased foil.
2. On medium heat, add butter to your double boiler and let it melt.
3. Chop up the white chocolate squares and add in. Then, pour in the sweetened condensed milk, stirring constantly with a whisk until well-blended.
4. Pour and spread the mixture evenly into the pan.
5. Pour the cranberry jam into a piping bag and squeeze the jam over the top of fudge in a swirling motion.
6. Refrigerate the fudge so it sets properly. Once cool, cut into squares and enjoy!

Butter Pecan Fudge

Ingredients

- 1 cup toasted shelled pecans
- ½ cup butter
- ½ cup brown sugar
- ½ cup white sugar
- ½ cup heavy whipping cream
- 1 teaspoon vanilla extract
- 2 cups powdered sugar
- Dash of salt

Instructions

How to toast pecans: Preheat the oven to 350 degrees. Place pecans in a single layer on a baking sheet. Once oven is heated, place baking sheet in the oven for about 5 minutes.

1. Grease an 8" x 8" pan with butter. Set aside.

2. Add confectioners' sugar to a medium mixing bowl. Set aside.

3. In a medium size pot or sauce pan, combine butter, white sugar, brown sugar, heavy whipping cream and salt. Heat over medium heat until it reaches a boil. Then stir for exactly 5 minutes while boiling.

4. Remove the pan from the heat and stir in powdered sugar, vanilla and pecans.

5. Pour and spread the mixture into pan. Let fudge cool for preferably 24 hours. Once cool, cut into small squares and serve.

Cappuccino Fudge

Ingredients

- 1 tablespoon heavy cream
- 2 tablespoons instant coffee
- 2 cups milk or dark chocolate chips
- 1 can milk or dark chocolate frosting
- 2 cups white chocolate chips
- 1 can vanilla canned frosting

Instructions

1. Line a 7" x 7" baking pan with lightly greased foil. Set aside.

2. Heat up the chocolate chips in the microwave until they are melted.

3. Heat up the heavy cream in a bowl for 15 seconds, remove and pour in the instant coffee. Then set the bowl aside so you can let the coffee dissolve.

4. Microwave the container of chocolate frosting for 45 seconds, then remove and stir. Repeat until the frosting is melted.

5. Pour melted frosting into the melted chocolate chips. Then spread the mixture into the pan and refrigerate so it can set.

6. Heat the container of vanilla frosting in the microwave the same way and then add in the heavy cream coffee mixture.

7. Melt the white chocolate chips in a bowl until melted and then combine and stir the coffee frosting into the melted white chocolate.

8. Pour the new mixture on top of the refrigerated chocolate layer. Let entire pan of fudge cool for 4 hours or more before cutting.

Cinnamon Sugar Fudge

Ingredients
- 3 cups white chocolate chips
- 14 ounces sweetened condensed milk
- 1/2 tsp vanilla extract
- 1 1/4 tsp cinnamon + a pinch
- Pinch of sugar

Instructions

1. Line an 8" x 8" baking pan with parchment paper. Set aside.

2. Add chocolate chips and sweetened condensed milk into a sauce pan and melt over low heat, while stirring.

3. Once it's melted, remove the pan from heat and add in the vanilla and cinnamon.

4. Stir, then pour and spread the mixture into the baking pan.

5. Sprinkle a little cinnamon and sugar over the top of the fudge.

6. Refrigerate for a few hours until its cool. Once cool, cut into small squares and enjoy!

Cherry Fudge With Dark Chocolate

Ingredients

- 2 1/2 cup white chocolate
- 7 ounce jar of marshmallow crème
- 3/4 cup butter
- 1 cup sugar
- 3/4 cup heavy cream
- 1 tablespoon cherry gelatin
- 1/2 cup dried cherries
- 10 ounces of melted dark chocolate
- Pinch of salt

Instructions

1. Line a 9" x 9" pan with parchment paper. Set aside.

2. Combine butter, sugar, cream and a pinch of salt in large saucepan. Melt and bring to a boil over medium high heat. Once boiling, add in cherry gelatin. Continue to boil for 5 minutes. Remove the pan from heat.

3. Combine white chocolate and marshmallow crème in a large mixing bowl. Pour the hot mixture over this and beat with a whisk until melted and smooth.

4. Use a spatula to fold in the dried up cherries.

5. Pour and spread mixture into pan. Pour the melted dark chocolate on the cherry fudge and refrigerate for a few hours until cool and set. Cut into small squares and serve.

Rocky Road Fudge

Ingredients

- 12 ounces semi-sweet chocolate chips
- 14 ounces sweetened condensed milk
- 1 teaspoon vanilla extract
- 3 cups miniature marshmallows
- 1 1/2 cups chopped walnuts

Instructions

1. Line a 13" x 9" pan with lightly greased foil. Set aside.

2. Combine chocolate chips and sweetened condensed milk a large bowl. Microwave on high for 1 minute and stir. Then, stir in vanilla extract and fold in marshmallows and nuts.

3. Pour and press fudge into the pan. Refrigerate until completely cool. Cut into small squares and serve.

Chocolate Raspberry Truffle Fudge

Ingredients

- 5 cups semi-sweet chocolate chips
- 14 ounces sweetened condensed milk
- 1 1/2 teaspoons vanilla extract
- salt to taste
- 1/4 cup heavy cream
- 1/4 cup raspberry flavored liqueur

Instructions

1. Line 9" x 9" pan with lightly greased wax paper. Set aside.

2. Combine 3 cups chocolate chips and the sweetened condensed milk into a microwave-safe bowl. Microwave the mixture until chocolate is melted. Stir occasionally so that the chocolate does not burn. After it is melted, add and stir in the vanilla and salt.

3. Pour and spread the mixture into the pan and let it cool.

4. Combine the heavy cream, liqueur, and 2 cups of chocolate chips into a different microwave-safe bowl. Heat the mixture until the chocolate melts – make sure to stir so it does not burn.

5. Cool the mixture to room temperature, then pour and spread over the fudge layer.

6. Refrigerate for a few hours until both layers are completely set. Once set, cut into squares and serve.

Coconut Chocolate Fudge With Almonds

Ingredients

Fudge
- 1 1/2 cups milk chocolate Hershey's Kisses
- 1 1/2 cups chocolate candy melts
- 14 ounces can sweetened condensed milk

Coconut
- 14 ounces bag sweetened shredded coconut
- 1 cup powdered sugar
- 1/2 cup + 1 tbsp. sweetened condensed milk

Chocolate Candy
- 20 whole raw almonds
- 1 cup chocolate candy melts

Instructions

1. Line a 9"x 9" pan with lightly greased parchment paper. Set aside.

2. Combine the Hershey's Kisses, the chocolate melting candy, and a whole can of sweetened condensed milk in a medium saucepan and melt over low heat, while stirring. Stir until melted.

3. Scrape and pour the fudge into the pan and set aside.

4. Combine and mix 1/2 cup + 1 tbsp. sweetened condensed milk, coconut, and confectioners' sugar in a large mixing bowl. If you don't have a stand mixer, you can use a hand mixer on the low setting.

5. On a piece of parchment paper that is the approximate size of the 9"x 9" pan, scrape out the

coconut mixture onto the paper and use a rubber spatula to press the coconut into a square the size of the dish. Invert the coconut square on top of the fudge and gently press down.

6. Sprinkle the almonds evenly over top of the coconut layer.

7. Melt the remaining chocolate in the microwave for 1 minute. Stir until melted and pour as evenly as possible over the almonds.

8. Refrigerate fudge for 4 to 6 hours, so that it sets. Once cool, cut into 1 inch squares and serve.

Candy Cane Fudge

Ingredients

- 3 cups of white chocolate chips
- 14 ounces sweetened condensed milk
- 1/2 teaspoon peppermint extract
- 8 crushed candy canes
- 2/3 cup mini semi-sweet chocolate chips

Instructions

1. Line an 8" x 8" square pan with lightly greased parchment paper or foil. Set aside.

2. In a medium saucepan, combine the white chocolate chips and sweetened condensed milk in over medium heat. Stir until melted. Once melted, remove the pan from heat and stir in the peppermint extract and candy canes.

3. Pour and spread evenly into the square pan. Top with chocolate chips and gently swirl them into the fudge with a knife. Sprinkle more crushed candy cane pieces on top.

4. Let the fudge chill for a few hours to set. Once cool, cut into small squares.

Spicy Mexican Chocolate Fudge

Ingredients

- 3 cups milk chocolate chips
- 1 can sweetened condensed milk
- 1 teaspoon vanilla extract
- 1 teaspoon cinnamon
- 1/4 teaspoon cayenne pepper

Instructions

1. Line an 8" x 8" pan with foil or parchment paper.
2. Melt the chocolate and the sweetened condensed milk over medium-low heat and stir.
3. Add in the vanilla, cinnamon and cayenne pepper.
4. Once everything is well-blended, pour the fudge into the pan.
5. Refrigerate the fudge for a few hours so it can properly set. Once cool, remove the fudge from the pan, cut into small squares and enjoy!

Butterscotch Fudge

Ingredients

- 1 1/2 cups sugar
- 2/3 cup evaporated milk
- 2 tablespoons butter
- 1/4 teaspoon salt
- 2 cups miniature marshmallows
- 1 2/3 cups butterscotch chips
- 1 teaspoon vanilla extract
- 1/2 cup chopped nuts

Instructions

1. Line an 8" x 8" pan with lightly greased foil. Set aside.

2. In a medium heavy saucepan, combine sugar, evaporated milk, butter and salt. Stir as you bring the mixture to a full boil over medium heat. Stir for another 5 minutes while it boils and then remove the pan from heat.

3. Add and stir in marshmallows, butterscotch chips, nuts and vanilla. Stir until marshmallows are melted.

4. Pour and spread the fudge into the pan. Refrigerate for 3 hours or until firm. When it's completely cool, remove from the pan and cut into squares.

Classic Hot Fudge Sauce

Ingredients

- 12 ounces evaporated milk
- 12 ounces semi-sweet chocolate chips
- 1/2 cup sugar
- 1 tablespoon butter
- 1 teaspoon vanilla extract

Instructions

1. Combine milk, chocolate chips and sugar in a medium saucepan.

2. Heat to boiling over medium heat – make sure you keep stirring so it does not burn.

3. Remove the pan from heat, and stir in the butter and vanilla.

4. Serve warm over ice cream or any dessert of your choosing!

Chocolate Pretzel Fudge

Ingredients

- 3 cups semi-sweet chocolate chips
- 2 tablespoons unsalted butter, cubed
- 14 ounces sweetened condensed milk
- 1/2 teaspoon vanilla extract
- 1/8 teaspoon salt
- 2 1/2 cups chopped miniature pretzels

Instructions

1. Line an 8" x 8" pan with parchment paper - make sure there is excess paper extending over the edge of the pan. Set aside.

2. Combine butter, chocolate, condensed milk, vanilla, and salt in the top bowl of a double boiler or a medium bowl set over a pot of simmering water, if you don't have one.

3. Stir for 8 minutes until chocolate is melted and mixture is warm. Remove from heat and stir in 2 cups of chopped pretzels.

4. Pour and spread the fudge mixture into the pan and sprinkle the rest of the pretzels on top.

5. Cover the pan and let it cool in the refrigerator for about 2 to 3 hours. After its cool, remove the fudge from the pan. Cut into small squares and serve.

Chocolate Pomegranate Fudge

Ingredients

- 14 ounces sweetened condensed milk
- 3 cups semi-sweet chocolate chips
- Arils of 1 pomegranate (about 1 cup)

Instructions

1. Line a 9" x 9" pan with plastic wrap. Set aside.

2. Combine the sweetened condensed milk and chocolate chips in a small saucepan over medium low heat. Stir until mixture is melted.

3. Once melted, remove from the heat and fold in all but 1/4 cup of the arils.

4. Spread the fudge mixture into pan and press the remaining arils into the top of the fudge.

5. Refrigerate for a few hours. Once firm, cut into squares and serve.

Peanut Butter Fudge

Ingredients

- 1 cup creamy peanut butter
- 16 ounces powdered sugar
- 8 ounces unsalted butter
- 1 teaspoon vanilla extract

Instructions

1. Line an 8" x 8" pan with lightly greased parchment paper. Set aside.

2. In a microwave-safe bowl, add the butter and peanut butter and cover with plastic wrap. Heat in the microwave on high for 2 minutes.

3. Remove bowl from the microwave, stir, and microwave on high again for 2 minutes.

4. Carefully remove the bowl and stir in the vanilla and confectioners' sugar.

5. Pour and spread the fudge mixture into the pan in an even layer.

6. Cover the fudge with another piece of parchment paper and refrigerate for at least 2 hours. Once it's cool, cut into squares and enjoy!

Brown Sugar Fudge

Ingredients

- 1/2 cup + 2 tablespoons evaporated milk
- 2 cups brown sugar
- 3/4 cup unsalted butter, cubed
- 1/4 teaspoon salt
- 1/2 teaspoon vanilla extract
- 1 3/4 cup powdered sugar, sifted
- 3/4 cup toasted walnuts, chopped (optional)

Instructions

1. In a dense saucepan, combine evaporated milk, brown sugar, butter, and salt. Bring to a boil over medium flame. Stir until melted and smooth.

2. Remove from heat and pour into a large mixing bowl. Add in the vanilla and blend with a hand mixer.

3. Add in the confectioners' sugar in small portions while continuing to beat with the mixer until well-blended. Add the walnuts and mix until walnuts are just covered.

4. Pour and spread the fudge into an ungreased 8" x 8" pan.

5. Refrigerate for 1 hour or until firm. Once firm, cut into squares and serve.

Popcorn Fudge

Ingredients

- 1 package semisweet chocolate chips
- 1 can sweetened condensed milk
- 2 tablespoons butter or margarine
- 4 cups popped popcorn
- 1 cup almonds (optional)
- 1 teaspoon vanilla extract

Instructions

1. Line a 9" x 13" pan with lightly greased wax paper. Set aside.

2. Over low heat, combine chocolate chips, condensed milk and butter in a large saucepan. Stir until melted and smooth.

3. Once melted, remove from heat and stir in popcorn, nuts and vanilla.

4. Pour and spread fudge evenly in the pan.

5. Chill for several hours until firm. Remove from pan and cut into small squares.

Hot Chocolate Recepies

Creamy Hot Cocoa

Serves 4

What you'll need:

1/3 cup unsweetened cocoa powder
3/4 cup white sugar
1 pinch salt
1/3 cup boiling water
3 1/2 cups milk
3/4 teaspoon vanilla extract
1/2 cup half-and-half cream

What to do:

Combine the cocoa, sugar and pinch of salt in a saucepan. Blend in the boiling water. Bring this mixture to an easy boil while you stir. Simmer and stir for about 2 minutes. Watch that it doesn't scorch. Stir in 3 1/2 cups of milk and heat until very hot, but do not boil! Remove from heat and add vanilla. Divide between 4 mugs. Add the cream to the mugs of cocoa to cool it to drinking temperature.

Hot Cocoa Powder Mix

Serves 45

What you'll need:

10 cups dry milk powder
4 3/4 cups sifted confectioners' sugar
1 3/4 cups unsweetened cocoa powder
1 3/4 cups powdered non-dairy creamer

What to do:

In a large mixing bowl, combine milk powder, confectioner's sugar, cocoa powder, and creamer. Stir till thoroughly combined. Store cocoa mixture in an airtight container. Makes about 15 cups mix, or enough for about 45 servings.

For 1 serving, place 1/3 cup cocoa mixture in a coffee cup or mug, and add 3/4 cup boiling water. Stir to dissolve. Top with dollop of whipped cream or a few marshmallows, if desired.

Creamy Hot Chocolate

Serves 2 Quarts

What you'll need:

1 (14 ounce) can EAGLE BRAND® Sweetened Condensed Milk
1/2 cup unsweetened cocoa
1 1/2 teaspoons vanilla extract
1/8 teaspoon salt
6 1/2 cups hot water
Mini marshmallows (optional)

What to do:

In large saucepan over medium heat, combine sweetened condensed milk, cocoa, vanilla and salt; mix well. Slowly stir in water. Heat through, stirring occasionally. Do not boil. Top with marshmallows, (optional). Store covered in refrigerator.

Easy Mexican Hot Chocolate

Serves 2

What you'll need:

3 tablespoons instant hot chocolate mix
1 tablespoon chocolate syrup
1/2 teaspoon ground cinnamon
1 pinch chili powder
1/4 cup milk
3/4 cup boiling water

What to do:

In a large mug, mix the hot chocolate mix, chocolate syrup, cinnamon, and chili powder. Pour in the milk. Add the boiling water and stir.

Candy Cane Cocoa

Serves 4

What you'll need:

4 cups milk
3 (1 ounce) squares semisweet chocolate, chopped
4 peppermint candy canes, crushed
1 cup whipped cream
4 small peppermint candy canes

What to do:

In a saucepan, heat milk until hot, but not boiling. Whisk in the chocolate and the crushed peppermint candies until melted and smooth. Pour hot cocoa into four mugs, and garnish with whipped cream. Serve each with a candy cane stirring stick.

Microwave Hot Chocolate

Serves 3

What you'll need:

3 cups milk
1/3 cup semisweet chocolate, grated
1 tablespoon white sugar
1/2 teaspoon ground cinnamon
1 egg

What to do:

Put milk into a microwave-safe container and cook on High in microwave for 2 minutes. Mix in chocolate, sugar, and cinnamon. In a small bowl, whisk an egg until smooth, then mix it into the chocolate mixture.

Return to microwave and cook on High for 3 to 4 minutes or until foamy (be careful not to let it boil.) Whisk until smooth and pour into 3 mugs. Garnish with a sprinkle of cinnamon if desired.

Triple Rush Hot Chocolate

Serves 2

What you'll need:

1/2 cup semisweet chocolate chips
1/2 cup milk
1/4 teaspoon ground cinnamon
1 dash hot chili powder
1 teaspoon instant coffee granules
1/2 cup cold milk

What to do:

Combine the chocolate chips and milk in a glass or plastic dish, and microwave on high, stirring every 20 to 30 seconds, until melted and smooth. Mix in the coffee, cinnamon, and hot chili powder until the instant coffee has dissolved. Stir in the cold milk. Strain into 2 mugs. Thin with additional milk, if desired.

Vegan Hot Chocolate

Serves 2

What you'll need:

2 1/2 cups soy milk
3 tablespoons white sugar
3 tablespoons cocoa powder
1/2 teaspoon salt
1/2 teaspoon vanilla extract
1 pinch ground cinnamon
1 pinch cayenne pepper

What to do:

Bring the soy milk, sugar, cocoa powder, salt, vanilla extract, cinnamon, and cayenne pepper to a simmer in a saucepan over medium-high heat. Remove from the heat and whisk until frothy. Serve immediately.

Italian Hot Chocolate

Serves 2

What you'll need:

3 tablespoons cocoa powder
1 1/2 tablespoons white sugar
1 1/2 cups milk
2 tablespoons milk
1 tablespoon cornstarch

What to do:

Mix the cocoa powder and sugar together in a small saucepan. Stir the 1 1/2 cups milk into the saucepan until the sugar has dissolved. Place over low heat; slowly bring the mixture to a low simmer.

Whisk 2 tablespoons of milk together with the cornstarch in a small cup; slowly whisk the cornstarch slurry into the cocoa mixture. Continue cooking, whisking continually, until the hot chocolate reaches a pudding-like thickness, 2 to 3 minutes.

Peanut Buttercup Hot Chocolate

Serves 1

What you'll need:

1 (1 ounce) envelope instant hot chocolate mix
 2 teaspoons creamy peanut butter
What to do:

In a mug, prepare chocolate mix as directed on package. Stir in 1 or 2 teaspoons peanut butter.

Spiced Hot Chocolate

Serves 6

What you'll need:

6 cups skim milk
3 tablespoons unsweetened cocoa powder
3 tablespoons white sugar
1 teaspoon vanilla extract
1 teaspoon cinnamon
1/2 teaspoon chili powder
1/4 teaspoon ground nutmeg
1/4 teaspoon ground cloves

What to do:

Heat the milk in a saucepan over medium-low heat until lukewarm; stir the cocoa powder and sugar into the warmed milk until dissolved. Add the vanilla, cinnamon, chili powder, nutmeg, and cloves.

Heat another 5 minutes, stirring occasionally.

Mayan Hot Chocolate

Serves 1

What you'll need:

1 cup milk
3 tablespoons instant hot chocolate mix
1 teaspoon ground cinnamon
1 pinch cayenne pepper

What to do:

Mix the hot chocolate mix, cinnamon, and cayenne pepper together in a mug.

Pour the milk into a glass measuring cup; heat in microwave on High until it begins to boil, about 2 minutes. Slowly pour over the mixture in the mug, stirring with a small whisk as you pour. Enjoy immediately.

Homestyle Hot Cocoa

Serves 4

What you'll need:

1/2 cup white sugar
1/3 cup unsweetened cocoa powder
1/8 teaspoon ground cinnamon
1 pinch salt
1/3 cup boiling water
3 cups milk
1 cup half-and-half, divided
3/4 teaspoon vanilla extract
8 large marshmallows (optional)

What to do:

Whisk together sugar, cocoa powder, cinnamon, and salt in a saucepan; stir in boiling water. Whisk until sugar is dissolved.

Bring cocoa mixture to a simmer over medium-high heat, stirring constantly, about 2 minutes; stir milk and 1/2 cup half-and-half into water mixture. Cook and stir just until hot, about 2 minutes. Remove saucepan from heat; stir in remaining half-and-half and vanilla extract. Divide cocoa into mugs, top with marshmallows, and serve.

Creamy Vegan Hot Cocoa

Serves 1

What you'll need:

3 tablespoons canned coconut milk
1/2 teaspoon vanilla extract
3 tablespoons white sugar
4 1/2 teaspoons cocoa powder
1 dash ground cinnamon
1 cup boiling water

What to do:

Stir together coconut milk, vanilla extract, sugar, cocoa powder, and cinnamon in a large mug. Add boiling water and stir until the sugar has dissolved.

Whipped Hot Chocolate

Serves 4

What you'll need:

1 cup milk
1/3 cup white sugar
2 tablespoons sweetened cocoa powder
1 teaspoon vanilla extract
1 pinch salt
2 (1 ounce) squares semisweet baking chocolate, broken into pieces
1 cup heavy cream
What to do:

Heat milk in a small saucepan over low heat until the milk begins to steam. Whisk in the sugar, cocoa powder, vanilla extract, and salt until dissolved. Stir in the chocolate until melted. Remove saucepan from heat, and allow to cool slightly.

Beat the heavy cream in large mixing bowl with an electric mixer until stiff peaks form. Gently fold the whipped cream into the hot chocolate. Serve immediately.

Thin Mint Cocoa

Serves 4

What you'll need:

1/2 cup white sugar
1/4 cup hot cocoa mix
1 dash salt
1/3 cup hot water
4 cups whole milk
1 teaspoon vanilla extract
1 teaspoon peppermint extract

What to do:

Mix the sugar, cocoa mix, and salt into the water in a saucepan until completely dissolved. Bring the mixture to a boil; cook and stir at a boil for 2 minutes. Stir the milk, vanilla extract, and peppermint extract through the mixture. Continue cooking until hot, but do not bring to a boil. Serve hot.

Chocolate Bar Hot Chocolate

Serves 1

What you'll need:

1 (1.55 ounce) bar milk chocolate candy bar, chopped
2/3 cup milk, or more to taste
1 pinch ground cinnamon (optional)
What to do:

Place chocolate pieces in a saucepan over medium-low heat; add milk and whisk constantly until chocolate is melted and well blended, about 5 minutes. Whisk in cinnamon. Remove from heat; add more milk if desired. Serve in a mug.

Pumpkin Spice Hot Chocolate

Serves 2

What you'll need:

1/2 cup milk
1/3 cup heavy whipping cream
1/4 cup milk chocolate chips
1 teaspoon cocoa powder
1 1/2 teaspoons pumpkin puree
1/4 teaspoon pumpkin pie spice
1/4 cup whipped cream
1 pinch ground cinnamon (optional)
1 pinch ground nutmeg (optional)

What to do:

Whisk milk, cream, chocolate chips, and cocoa powder together in a saucepan over medium heat until chocolate chips are melted and hot chocolate is smooth, 3 to 5 minutes. Stir in pumpkin puree and pumpkin pie spice until fully incorporated.

Pour hot chocolate into 2 mugs. Top with whipped cream; sprinkle cinnamon and nutmeg over whipped cream.

Kocoa Klastch Blend

Serves 24

What you'll need:

2 pounds confectioners' sugar, sifted
4 cups French vanilla flavored powdered coffee creamer
2 cups Dutch process cocoa powder
2 tablespoons dried orange zest
1 tablespoon ground cinnamon
1 teaspoon ground anise seed

What to do:

In a large bowl, stir together the confectioners' sugar, coffee creamer, cocoa, orange zest, cinnamon and anise seed. Store in an airtight container, or separate into smaller jars for gift giving.

To prepare, mix 1/4 cup of the cocoa mix with 1 1/2 cups of hot milk or boiling water.

Chocolate Lover's Hot Chocolate

Serves 3

What you'll need:

2 1/2 cups milk
1/2 teaspoon brown sugar
1/2 teaspoon maple syrup
1/2 teaspoon vanilla extract
1/2 teaspoon honey
3 1/2 tablespoons unsweetened cocoa powder
1/2 cup milk

What to do:

Heat 2 1/2 cups milk in a saucepan over medium heat until steaming, about 5 minutes. Stir in brown sugar, maple syrup, honey, and vanilla extract. Bring to boil and stir in cocoa powder. Remove from heat and add the remaining 1/2 cup milk. Return saucepan over heat and simmer until heated through, about 2 minutes more. Ladle into cups to serve.

Mexican-Style Hot Chocolate

Serves 12

What you'll need:

1 1/2 cups cold water
1/2 cup white sugar
1/4 cup unsweetened cocoa powder
2 tablespoons all-purpose flour
1 teaspoon ground cinnamon
1/4 teaspoon ground cloves
1/4 teaspoon salt
6 cups whole milk
1 tablespoon vanilla extract

What to do:

Whisk cold water, sugar, cocoa powder, flour, cinnamon, cloves, and salt in a saucepan until smooth. Place over low heat; bring to a simmer, whisking constantly, until mixture is thickened and hot, about 4 minutes. Stir in milk; heat until hot chocolate just forms bubbles around the edge. Mix vanilla extract into hot chocolate. Blend until smooth with an immersion blender to make the drink slightly frothy.

Champurrado

Serves 12

What you'll need:

1 1/2 cups water
1 cinnamon stick
1 whole clove
1 pod star anise (optional)
4 1/4 cups milk
2 tablets Mexican chocolate (such as Chocolate Ibarra®)
3/4 cup pinole (coarse ground maize flour)
1 pinch crushed piloncillo (Mexican brown sugar cone), or more to taste

What to do:

Bring water, cinnamon stick, clove, and star anise to a boil in a saucepan; remove from heat and allow spices to steep until water is fragrant, about 10 minutes. Strain.

Heat milk, chocolate, and pinole in another saucepan over medium heat, whisking until chocolate is dissolved and liquid is thickened, about 10 minutes. Remove from heat and add piloncillo; let rest until sugar is dissolved, about 5 minutes more. Pour cinnamon water into chocolate mixture and stir to combine.

Coconut Hot Cocoa

Serves 1

What you'll need:

1 cup vanilla-flavored coconut milk beverage (such as Silk®)
2 tablespoons cocoa powder
1 tablespoon white sugar
1/4 teaspoon vanilla extract
1/4 teaspoon ground cinnamon

What to do:

Stir coconut milk beverage, cocoa powder, sugar, vanilla extract, and cinnamon together in a saucepan over medium heat until cocoa and sugar are completely dissolved and mixture is heated through, 5 to 10 minutes. Pour hot cocoa into a mug.

Hawaiian Hot Chocolate

Serves 4

What you'll need:

3 cups half-and-half
1 cup 2% milk
1/2 cup white sugar
1/2 cup unsweetened cocoa powder
1 tablespoon vanilla extract
1 tablespoon coconut extract
1/2 teaspoon kosher salt
1/2 cup whipped cream, or more to taste
1/4 cup toasted, shredded coconut

What to do:

Whisk half-and-half, milk, sugar, and cocoa powder in a saucepan over medium-high heat until cocoa and sugar dissolve. Remove from heat when mixture begins to steam, 5 to 10 minutes.

Whisk vanilla extract, coconut extract, and salt into cocoa mixture. Pour into glasses and top each with whipped cream and toasted coconut.

Frozen Hot Chocolate

Serves 2

What you'll need:

1 cup crushed ice
1 cup milk
1 (1 ounce) envelope instant hot chocolate mix
What to do:

Blend ice, milk, and hot chocolate mix together in a blender until smooth.

Smooth Hot Chocolate

Serves 4

What you'll need:

1 cup nonfat dry milk powder
5 tablespoons white sugar
3 tablespoons baking cocoa
1/8 teaspoon ground cinnamon, or more to taste
1 dash salt
3 cups boiling water

What to do:

Stir milk powder, sugar, cocoa, cinnamon, and salt together in a saucepan. Pour boiling water over the milk powder mixture; stir until mixture is dissolved into the liquid.

Orange Hot Chocolate

Serves 1

What you'll need:

1 cup milk
1 (1 ounce) envelope instant hot cocoa mix (such as Swiss Miss®)
1/4 cup orange juice
1/8 teaspoon ground cinnamon

What to do:

Heat milk in a saucepan over high heat; whisk hot cocoa mix into milk until completely dissolved.

Continue whisking for 1 minute, reduce heat to medium, and gradually stir in orange juice. Sprinkle cinnamon over the top and stir. Pour hot chocolate into a mug.

Dark Chocolate Hot Cocoa

Serves 1

What you'll need:

1 cup whole milk
1 1/2 teaspoons brown sugar, or to taste
2 ounces dark chocolate (such as Moser Roth® 85% Dark Chocolate), or to taste
1 tablespoon heavy whipping cream, or more to taste
1 pinch ground cinnamon, or more to taste

What to do:

Heat milk in a saucepan over medium heat until just before boiling, 3 to 4 minutes. Add brown sugar and stir until dissolved, about 1 minute. Stir dark chocolate into milk until melted, 2 to 3 minutes. Remove saucepan from heat and stir cream and cinnamon into milk mixture.

Cinnamon Hot Chocolate Mix

Serves 2

What you'll need:

1 3/4 cups non-fat dry milk powder
1 cup granular no-calorie sucralose sweetener (such as Splenda®)
1/2 cup non-dairy creamer
1/2 cup baking cocoa
1/2 teaspoon ground cinnamon
1 cup miniature marshmallows

What to do:

Combine milk powder, sweetener, creamer, cocoa, and cinnamon in a bowl; add marshmallows and mix. Store in an airtight container in a cool dry place for up to 3 months.

To prepare hot chocolate: Dissolve about 3 tablespoons hot chocolate mix in hot milk.

Nutella Hot Chocolate

Serves 1

What you'll need:

3 tablespoons Nutella
1 1/3 cups milk
What to do:

Put Nutella and 1/3 cup milk in small saucepan over medium heat.
Whisk until blended.
Add remaining milk, increase heat to medium-high, and whisk until hot and frothy.

Ultra-Rich Hot Chocolate

Serves 4

What you'll need:

4 cups milk
1/4 cup unsweetened cocoa powder
1/2 cup sugar
4 ounces bittersweet chocolate or 4 ounces semisweet chocolate, chopped
1 pinch salt
Miniature marshmallow
Whipped cream (optional)

What to do:

Bring milk, cocoa powder and sugar to simmer in heavy large saucepan over medium-high heat, whisking frequently.

Add chocolate; whisk until melted and smooth.

Add salt; bring to simmer, whisking constantly until frothy.

Ladle into 4 mugs.

Sprinkle with marshmallows or dollop of whipped cream.

Caramel Hot Chocolate

Serves 2

What you'll need:

2 cups chocolate milk
2 tablespoons caramel topping
Frozen whipped topping, thawed, if desired (optional)
Pecans, chopped, if desired (optional)
What to do:

Stir milk and caramel in a 1 qt saucepan until well blended.
Heat over medium-high heat, stirring frequently until hot.
Pour into 4 mugs.
Garnish with whipped topping and pecans.

New England Hot Chocolate

Serves 4

What you'll need:

1/4 cup sugar
1 tablespoon baking cocoa
1/8 teaspoon salt
1/4 cup hot water
1 tablespoon butter or 1 tablespoon margarine
4 cups milk
1 teaspoon maple flavoring
1 teaspoon vanilla extract
12 large marshmallows

What to do:

In a large saucepan, combine sugar, cocoa, and salt.
Stir in hot water and butter; bring to a boil.
Add the milk, maple flavoring, vanilla and 8 marshmallows.
Heat through, stirring occasionally, until marshmallows melt.
Pour into mugs and top each with a marshmallow.

Moscow Hot Chocolate

Serves 1

What you'll need:

1 ounce vanilla vodka
3/4 ounce amaretto liqueur
1 tablespoon instant hot chocolate powder
4 ounces milk, hot
What to do:

Pour vanilla vodka, amaretto, and hot chocolate mix into a coffee mug.
Pour in the hot milk and stir to blend.

Brazilian Hot Chocolate

Serves 6

What you'll need:

2 ounces baking chocolate
1/4 cup sugar
1/4 teaspoon salt
1/4 teaspoon ground cinnamon
3 teaspoons instant coffee
2 cups hot water
2 cups hot milk
1 1/2 teaspoons vanilla extract

What to do:

In a double boiler, melt the chocolate, then stir in the sugar, salt cinnamon and instant coffee.

Remove the top of the double boiler and warm over direct heat, adding ¼ c of the hot water, stirring for ½ minute.

Then, stirring constantly, add in the rest of the hot water and milk.

Remove from heat and stir in the vanilla.

Serve while still hot.

Belgian Hot Chocolate

Serves 6

What you'll need:

1 quart half-and-half or 1 quart whole milk
8 ounces bittersweet chocolate or 8 ounces semisweet chocolate, finely chopped
4 ounces good milk chocolate, finely chopped
Tiny pinch salt
1/2 teaspoon ground cinnamon

What to do:

Warm about one-third of the half-and-half or milk, with the chopped chocolates and salt, stirring until the chocolate is melted.

Whisk in the remaining half-and-half or milk, heating until the mixture is warmed through. Add the cinnamon.

Use a hand-held blender, or a whisk, and mix the hot chocolate until it's completely smooth. Serve very warm. Enjoy!

Spanish Hot Chocolate

Serves 4

What you'll need:

1⁄2 lb good-quality semisweet chocolate (or bittersweet)
4 cups milk
2 tablespoons sugar
1 teaspoon cinnamon
What to do:

If your chocolate is in a bar form, chop or grate. Solid bars do not melt well.

Put chocolate, milk and sugar in a heavy saucepan over low heat. Whisk slowly until the chocolate melts and sugar dissolves.

When it is smooth and steamy, put into mugs and top with a little cinnamon.

French Style Hot Chocolate

Serves 5

What you'll need:

4 ounces unsweetened chocolate pieces
4 cups milk
3/4 cup half-and-half
1/2 cup sugar
1/2 teaspoon ground nutmeg
1/2 teaspoon ground cinnamon
1/4 teaspoon ground allspice
1 teaspoon vanilla
1/2 teaspoon almond extract
1/2 cup heavy cream, whipped for topping

What to do:

Melt chocolate in 1 cup of milk, over low heat, stirring constantly.

Gradually add remaining milk and half and half, followed by remaining ingredients, except vanilla and almond extract.

Cook over medium heat, stirring constantly, until completely heated.

Stir in vanilla and almond extract.

Serve with whipped cream and sprinkle with nutmeg if desired.

Hot Spiced New England Cider

Serves 4

What you'll need:

6 cups apple-pear cider (or Apple Cider)
1/4 cup maple syrup (1/2 cup with Apple Cider)
2 cinnamon Sticks (Cassia, plus an additional cinnamon stick for each person)
6 whole cloves
6 allspice berries
1 drop lemon juice
What to do:

Combine cider, syrup, lemon juice, and spices and heat thoroughly, but do not boil.
Remove spices.
Put a cinnamon stick in each cup to drink through and serve hot.

Hazelnut Hot Chocolate

Serves 1

What you'll need:

3/4 cup hot water
1/4 cup hot milk
2 teaspoons hazelnut instant coffee
1 teaspoon baking cocoa
1 tablespoon dark brown sugar
1 tablespoon whipped cream (optional)
What to do:

Combine water, milk, instant coffee and cocoa in large mug; stir until coffee and cocoa are dissolved.
Stir in sugar.
Top with whipped cream.
Serve hot.

Part 2

Chocolate Truffle Cheesecake

"This chocolate cheesecake is a huge success with 10 grams of fat a slice, due to the reduced-fat cream cheese, pureed cottage cheese, cocoa powder and high-quality chocolate."

Serving: 16 | Ready in: 5h30m

Ingredients

- 1 cup chocolate wafer crumbs, (about 20 wafers)
- 1 tbsp. brown sugar
- 1 tbsp. canola oil
- 1 tsp. instant coffee granules, dissolved in 2 tsps. hot water
- 24 oz. 1% cottage cheese, (3 cups)
- 12 oz. reduced-fat cream cheese, (1½ cups), cut into pieces
- 1 cup packed brown sugar
- ½ cup granulated sugar
- ¾ cup unsweetened cocoa powder
- ¼ cup cornstarch
- 1 large egg
- 2 large egg whites
- 2 tbsps. instant coffee granules, dissolved in 2 tbsps. hot water
- 2 tsps. vanilla extract
- ¼ tsp. salt
- 2 oz. bittersweet (not unsweetened) chocolate, melted

- 16 chocolate-covered coffee beans, (optional)

Direction

- Prepare by preheating the oven at 325°F. For the water bath, put a kettle of water on to the heat. Spritz cooking spray on a 9-inch springform pan. Using a double thickness of foil, wrap the outside bottom of pan.
- For the crust, mix using your fingers or fork the coffee, oil, sugar and crumbs in a small bowl. Compress onto the base of pan.
- For the filling, blend cottage cheese using a food processor until smooth in texture, pausing one or two times to scrape sides. Put in cornstarch, cocoa, granulated sugar, brown sugar and cream cheese. Blend until smooth in texture. Put in and blend well chocolate, salt, vanilla, coffee, egg whites and egg. Put in the crust-lined pan.
- On a roasting pan add in adequate amount of water of the springform pan, about 1/2 inch up, then place the cheesecake.
- Put cheesecake inside the oven and bake for 50 minutes at until the edges have set and the center is still jiggly. Turn the oven's heat off. Use a knife sprayed with cooking spray and cautiously run it around the pan's edges. Partly open the oven door and let the cheesecake rest for 1 hour. Transfer to a wire rack from the water bath; take off foil. For 2 hours, let cake cool

to room temperature. Uncover and chill the cheesecake in the refrigerator.
• Decorate the cheesecake with coffee beans covered with chocolate before serving.

Nutrition Information
• Calories: 223 calories;
• Total Carbohydrate: 34 g
• Cholesterol: 25 mg
• Total Fat: 7 g
• Fiber: 2 g
• Protein: 9 g
• Sodium: 322 mg
• Sugar: 26 g
• Saturated Fat: 3 g

Chocolate Truffle Raspberry Cheesecake

"This recipe is so marvelous! I can't stop eating this cheesecake with a truffle layer and raspberry-swirl on its top no matter how full I am."
Serving: 16 servings. | Prep: 45m | Ready in: 01h30m

Ingredients
• 2 cups cream-filled chocolate sandwich cookie crumbs

- 2 tbsps. butter, melted
- FILLING:
- 2 packages (8 oz. each) cream cheese, softened
- 3/4 cup sugar
- 1 cup white baking chips, melted and cooled
- 1/3 cup heavy whipping cream
- 3 tsps. vanilla extract
- 3 eggs, lightly beaten
- 3 tbsps. seedless raspberry jam
- TRUFFLE LAYER:
- 1-1/4 cups heavy whipping cream
- 1/3 cup sugar
- 2 cups (12 oz.) semisweet chocolate chips
- 3 tbsps. seedless raspberry jam
- Fresh raspberries and mint leaves, optional

Direction

- Mix butter and cookie crumbs in a big bowl. Place the mixture into a greased 9-inches springform pan, pressing it at its bottom with 1-inch up the sides of the pan; put aside.

- Whisk sugar and cream cheese in a big bowl until smooth. Stir in vanilla, melted chips, and cream. Beat in eggs at low speed until just incorporated. Pour the mixture all over the crust. Add teaspoonfuls of jam into the filling and swirl it using a knife. Place the springform pan on the baking sheet.

- Set the oven to 325°F. Bake the cake for 45-50 minutes until the center is nearly fixed. Let it cool for

10 minutes on a wire rack. Use a knife to loosen up its edges and let it cool for 60 more minutes.
- To make its truffle layer, combine sugar and cream in a small heavy saucepan. Place the pan over moderate heat and let it boil while stirring the mixture constantly. Remove the mixture from the heat after boiling and mix in jam and chips until smooth. Transfer the mixture into a bowl and store it in a fridge for 60 minutes until nearly-fixed. Whisk the mixture for 1-2 minutes until fluffy and light before pouring it all over the cheesecake. Store the cheesecake inside the fridge overnight.
- Style it up with mint and raspberries if you want.

Nutrition Information
- Calories: 527 calories
- Total Carbohydrate: 52 g
- Cholesterol: 108 mg
- Total Fat: 35 g
- Fiber: 2 g
- Protein: 6 g
- Sodium: 223 mg

Chocolate Turtle Cheesecake

"Your family and friends will surely love my own version of cheesecake!"
Serving: Makes 16 servings. | Prep: 15m | Ready in: 5h50m

Ingredients

- 1-1/2 cups crushed vanilla wafers (about 50)
- 3/4 cup chopped PLANTERS Pecans , divided
- 1/4 cup (1/2 stick) butter , melted
- 32 KRAFT Caramels
- 3 Tbsp. milk
- 4 pkg. (8 oz. each) PHILADELPHIA Cream Cheese , softened
- 1 cup sugar
- 1 cup BREAKSTONE'S or KNUDSEN Sour Cream
- 4   egg s
- 2 pkg. (4 oz. each) BAKER'S Semi-Sweet Chocolate , divided

Direction

- Combine butter, a half cup of nuts, and wafer crumbs and press the mixture at the bottom of a 13x9-inches pan. In a microwavable bowl, mix the milk and caramels, and heat it inside the microwave on Medium (50%) for 4-5 minutes, stirring the mixture every 2 minutes until well-blended and the caramels melted completely. Pour the mixture all over the crust, spreading it to within 1-inch of its edge. Set aside to cool.

- Whisk sugar and cream cheese until well-blended. Stir in sour cream. Beat in eggs, one at a time, whisking at low speed after every addition until just combined. Dissolve 7-oz. chocolate and add it into the cream cheese mixture. Spread the mixture all over the caramel layer.
- Let it bake inside the oven for 45-50 minutes until its center is nearly fixed. Set aside to cool completely. Store it inside the fridge for 4 hours. Top it with the remaining nuts and melted chocolate before serving.

Nutrition Information

- Calories: 540
- Total Carbohydrate: 45 g
- Cholesterol: 150 mg
- Total Fat: 38 g
- Fiber: 2 g
- Protein: 8 g
- Sodium: 350 mg
- Sugar: 37 g
- Saturated Fat: 20 g

Chocolate-Caramel Topped Cheesecake

""We prepare this dessert at our home on special occasions. The topping on the cheesecake tastes just like turtle candy.""

Serving: 12-14 servings. | Prep: 30m | Ready in: 01h15m

Ingredients

- 1-1/3 cups shortbread cookie crumbs
- 1/4 cup butter, melted
- FILLING:
- 3 packages (8 oz. each) cream cheese, softened
- 3/4 cup sugar
- 1/4 cup packed brown sugar
- 1 tbsp. vanilla extract
- 1/4 cup milk
- 2 tbsps. all-purpose flour
- 2 eggs, lightly beaten
- 1 egg yolk, lightly beaten
- TOPPING:
- 1/2 cup semisweet chocolate chips
- 1-1/2 tsps. shortening
- 1/2 cup coarsely chopped pecans, toasted
- 2 tbsps. caramel ice cream topping

Direction

- Mix butter and cookie crumbs in a small bowl. Then press onto the bottom of a 9-inch springform pan that is greased; reserve.

- Whip vanilla, sugars and cream cheese in a large bowl until smooth. Mix in flour and milk. Put in egg yolk and eggs, beating on low speed just until mixed. Put into crust. Put on a baking sheet.
- Place in the oven and bake for 45-50 minutes at 325°F or until middle is just set. Put on a wire rack to cool for 10 minutes. Gently run a knife around edge of pan to loosen; cool for 1 more hour. Cover and refrigerate for at least 6 hours or overnight.
- Remove side pan. Melt shortening and chocolate chips in a microwave; mix until smooth. Put pecans on top of cheesecake; then drizzle with caramel topping and chocolate mixture. Keep leftovers in the refrigerator.

Nutrition Information
- Calories: 283 calories
- Total Carbohydrate: 31 g
- Cholesterol: 74 mg
- Total Fat: 17 g
- Fiber: 1 g
- Protein: 4 g
- Sodium: 140 mg

Chocolate-Cherry Cheesecake Bars

""I've had this recipe for so long. I enjoy making it for Christmas and Valentine's Day. They beautiful bars also look festive for a shower or party.""
Serving: 15 bars. | Prep: 20m | Ready in: 40m

Ingredients

- 1 cup all-purpose flour
- 1/2 cup packed brown sugar
- 1/3 cup cold butter, cubed
- 1/2 cup finely chopped walnuts
- 1 package (8 oz.) cream cheese, softened
- 1/2 cup sugar
- 1/3 cup baking cocoa
- 1 large egg, lightly beaten
- 1/4 cup 2% milk
- 1/2 tsp. vanilla extract
- 1/2 cup chopped maraschino cherries
- Additional maraschino cherries, halved

Direction

- In a food processor, put the butter, brown sugar and flour; then cover and pulse until fine crumbs appear. Mix in walnuts. Reserve 3/4 cup for the topping.
- Onto the bottom of an 8-inch ungreased square baking dish, press leftover crumb mixture. Bake in the oven for 10 minutes until set at 350°F.

- In the meantime, whisk cocoa, sugar and cream cheese in a small bowl until it's smooth. Mix in vanilla, milk and egg; whisk using low speed until mixed. Mix in chopped cherries. Place on crust; dust with leftover crumb mixture.
- Bake in the oven for 20 to 25 minutes or until middle is set. Transfer on wire rack and cool for 1 hour. Keep in the refrigerator for 2 hours.
- Slice into bars; put cherry half on every top. Keep in the refrigerator.

Nutrition Information
- Calories: 227 calories
- Total Carbohydrate: 27 g
- Cholesterol: 42 mg
- Total Fat: 12 g
- Fiber: 1 g
- Protein: 4 g
- Sodium: 87 mg

Chocolate-Covered Cheesecake Squares

""Please your cheesecake craving with these bite-sized treats. Dipped in chocolate, these creamy and sweet delights are so well-loved at every party. Be careful though... one is not enough!""
Serving: 49 squares. | Prep: 55m | Ready in: 01h30m

Ingredients

- 1 cup graham cracker crumbs
- 1/4 cup finely chopped pecans
- 1/4 cup butter, melted
- FILLING:
- 2 packages (8 oz. each) cream cheese, softened
- 1/2 cup sugar
- 1/4 cup sour cream
- 2 large eggs, lightly beaten
- 1/2 tsp. vanilla extract
- COATING:
- 24 oz. semisweet chocolate, chopped
- 3 tbsps. shortening

Direction

- Use foil to line a 9-inch square baking pan and grease the foil. Mix in a bowl the butter, pecans and graham cracker crumbs. Then press into prepared pan; reserve.

- Whip sour cream, sugar and cream cheese in a large bowl until turn smooth. Put in vanilla and eggs; whisk

on low speed until mixed. Place over crust. Put in the oven and bake for 35-40 minutes at 325°F or until middle is just set. Put on a wire rack to cool. Then freeze overnight.
- Melt shortening and chocolate in a microwave; whisk until turn smooth. Slightly cool.
- Lift cheese out of pan using foil. Carefully peel off foil; slice cheesecake into 1-1/4 inch squares. Then work with a few pieces at a time for dipping; store remaining squares in the refrigerator until ready to dip.
- Fully dip squares using a toothpick, one at a time, in melted chocolate; let excess to drip off. Put on waxed paper-line baking sheets. Scoop additional chocolate over the tops if needed to cover. (Reheat chocolate if necessary to complete dipping). Allow to stand for 20 minutes or until set. Keep in an airtight container in the freezer or refrigerator.

Nutrition Information
- Calories: 141 calories
- Total Carbohydrate: 12 g
- Cholesterol: 22 mg
- Total Fat: 10 g
- Fiber: 1 g
- Protein: 2 g
- Sodium: 48 mg

Chocolate-Covered White Cheesecake

""A flavorful treat with a scoop of white chocolate center inside, which makes for an especially rich dessert suitable for celebrating New Year's. Serves when someone calls at holiday meals.""
Serving: 12-14 servings. | Prep: 30m | Ready in: 01h35m

Ingredients
- 1-1/2 cups chocolate wafer crumbs (about 27 wafers)
- 3 tbsps. butter, melted
- FILLING:
- 3 packages (8 oz. each) cream cheese, softened
- 1/2 cup sugar
- 1/4 cup heavy whipping cream
- 1 tsp. vanilla extract
- 3 large eggs, lightly beaten
- 1-1/2 cups vanilla or white chips, melted and cooled
- GLAZE:
- 2 cups (12 oz.) semisweet chocolate chips
- 1 cup heavy whipping cream
- 2 tbsps. butter
- 2 tbsps. sugar
- 1 cup vanilla or white chips, melted and cooled
- Striped chocolate kisses, optional
- Raspberries, optional

Direction

- Mix in a small bowl the butter and wafer crumbs; then press into the bottom of a 9-inch springform pan that was greased. Put the pan to a baking sheet. Place in the oven and bake for 10 minutes at 350°F. Transfer to a wire rack to cool.
- Whisk vanilla, cream, sugar and cream cheese in a large bowl until smooth. Put in eggs; whisk on low speed just until combined. Mix in melted vanilla chips. Put into crust. Put the pan on a double thickness of heavy-duty foil (about 16x16-inch). Tightly wrap foil around the pan.
- Put springform pan in a larger baking pan. Put 1-inch hot water to the larger pan. Place in the oven and bake for 65-70 minutes at 350°F or until middle is nearly set. Take out the pan from water bath. Transfer to a wire rack and cool for 10 minutes. Cautiously run a knife around the edge of pan to loosen; cool for 1 more hour. Refrigerate overnight.
- For glaze, put chocolate chips in a large bowl; reserve. Put the sugar, butter and cream in a heavy saucepan and bring to a boil over medium-high heat, whisking constantly. Then put over chocolate chips. Let it cool for 3 minutes. Stir until cool and smooth.
- Take off the sides of the pan. Place the glaze over the top and sides of cheesecake then spread. Keep in the refrigerator for 2 hours.
- Over cheesecake, drizzle melted vanilla chips. Decorate with raspberries and kisses if wished. Keep leftovers in the refrigerator.

Nutrition Information
- Calories: 479 calories
- Total Carbohydrate: 45 g
- Cholesterol: 96 mg
- Total Fat: 33 g
- Fiber: 2 g
- Protein: 6 g
- Sodium: 184 mg

Chocolate-Glazed Coconut Almond Cheesecake

""My concept was to create a cheesecake taste like my well-loved candy bar, which has almonds, coconut and chocolate. This cheesecake works in bite size too. Use a mini muffin lined with muffin liners, fill 3/4 full and bake for 15-17 minutes. Let it sit and fully cool before put almonds, coconut and chocolate on top.""
Serving: 12 servings. | Prep: 25m | Ready in: 01h10m

Ingredients
- 1-1/4 cups graham cracker crumbs
- 1/3 cup sweetened shredded coconut
- 1/3 cup finely chopped almonds
- 1/3 cup butter, melted
- FILLING:
- 3 packages (8 oz. each) cream cheese, softened

- 3/4 cup sugar
- 1 tbsp. coconut extract
- 3 large eggs, lightly beaten
- 1 cup sweetened shredded coconut
- GLAZE:
- 1 cup (6 oz.) semisweet chocolate chips
- 3/4 cup heavy whipping cream
- 1-1/2 tsps. vanilla extract
- Toasted coconut flakes and chopped almonds, optional

Direction

- Prepare the oven by preheating to 350°F. On a double thickness of heavy-duty foil (around 18-in.square), put a 9-inch greased springform pan. Tightly wrap foil on pan.
- Mix the almonds, coconut and cracker crumbs in a small bowl; mix in butter. Then press the bottom and 1-inch up the sides of the prepared pan. Transfer pan to a baking sheet. Bake in the oven for 12 minutes. Place on a wire rack and cool. Lower oven temperature to 325°F.
- Beat sugar and cream cheese in a big bowl until it turns smooth. Mix in the coconut extract. Put in eggs; whisk on low speed just until blended. Add coconut and fold. Place into crust. Transfer the springform pan to a large baking pan; put 1-inch of boiling water to bigger pan.

- Place in the preheated oven and bake for 45-55 minutes or until center is about set and top looks dull. Take springform pan from water bath; take off oil. Place cheesecake on a wire rack and cool for 10 minutes; use a knife to loosen edges from pan. Cool for 1 more hour. Keep in the refrigerator overnight.
- To make glaze, put the chocolate chips in a bowl that's small. Place cream in a small saucepan and make it boil. Place over chocolate; stir until smooth. Mix in vanilla. Let cool slightly to achieve a consistency that can easily be spread, whisking occasionally. Take out of pan. Put the glaze on cheesecake and spread. Keep in the refrigerator for 1 hour or until it has set. Place toasted coconut and/or almonds on top if you want.

Nutrition Information

- Calories: 543 calories
- Total Carbohydrate: 36 g
- Cholesterol: 149 mg
- Total Fat: 42 g
- Fiber: 2 g
- Protein: 8 g
- Sodium: 308 mg

Chocolate-Marbled Cheesecake Dessert

"This triple treat chocolate recipe features hot fudge, chocolate chips and baking cocoa! Small piece is enough to complete your holiday feast." Serving: 12-16 servings. | Prep: 25m | Ready in: 01h05m

Ingredients
- 1/2 cup butter, softened
- 1 cup sugar, divided
- 1 cup all-purpose flour
- 1/4 cup baking cocoa
- 1/4 tsp. salt
- 2 packages (8 oz. each) cream cheese, softened
- 2 eggs, lightly beaten
- 1 tsp. vanilla extract
- 1/2 cup hot fudge ice cream topping
- 1/4 cup semisweet chocolate chips, melted
- Milk chocolate or striped chocolate kisses, optional

Direction

• Cream 1/2 cup sugar and butter in a small bowl until fluffy and light. Mix the cocoa, salt and flour then slowly add to the creamed mixture; stir well. Press into an 8-in greased square baking dish. Put aside.

• Beat leftover sugar and cream cheese in a big bowl until smooth. Stir in vanilla and eggs. Beat on low speed just until combined. Take out 1 cup to a small bowl then beat in fudge topping. Spread 1 cup over the crust; spread remaining cream cheese mixture.

- Mix melted chips into the leftover fudge mixture; over cream cheese layer, drop it by teaspoonfuls. Use a knife to cut through the batter and to swirl.
- Place in the oven and bake for 40-45 minutes at 350 degrees or until an inserted toothpick in the middle comes out clean Transfer on a wire rack to cool. If desired, decorate with kisses. Chill in the refrigerator.

Nutrition Information

- Calories: 235 calories
- Total Carbohydrate: 27 g
- Cholesterol: 57 mg
- Total Fat: 13 g
- Fiber: 1 g
- Protein: 4 g
- Sodium: 158 mg

Chocolate-Topped Chocolate Cheesecake

"A hint of almond is added in the creamy chocolate filling of this luscious cheesecake."
Serving: 12 servings. | Prep: 20m | Ready in: 01h05m

Ingredients

- 1-1/4 cups graham cracker crumbs (about 20 squares)
- 1/2 cup sugar
- 1/4 cup baking cocoa
- 6 tbsps. butter, melted
- FILLING:
- 3 packages (8 oz. each) cream cheese, softened
- 3/4 cup sugar
- 3 large eggs, lightly beaten
- 1 cup (6 oz.) semisweet chocolate chips, melted
- 1 tsp. almond extract
- 1/2 tsp. vanilla extract
- TOPPING:
- 1/4 cup semisweet chocolate chips
- 1/3 cup heavy whipping cream
- 1 tbsp. honey

Direction

- Prepare the crust. Combine sugar, cracker crumbs and cocoa in a large bowl. Mix in butter until crumbly. Put the mixture in a greased 9-in. springform pan and press onto the bottom of the pan and 1-inch up its side. Set aside.

• Prepare the filling. Combine sugar and cream cheese in a small bowl. Beat until smooth. Drop in the eggs, beating on low speed just until blended. Mix in the melted chocolate and extracts and stir just until blended. Pour mixture into the prepared crust.

• Bake for 45 to 50 minutes at 350 degrees or until the center is almost set. Set pan aside on a wire rack to let it cool for 10 minutes. Loosen the edge by carefully running a knife around the pan's edge; cool for another 1 hour. Completely cool the cheesecake in the refrigerator.

• Prepare the topping. Combine cream, honey and chocolate chips in a small saucepan. Melt together over low heat and stir until smooth. Remove from the heat and let mixture cool for 5 minutes. Pour topping on top of the cheesecake then chill for at least 4 hours or until the topping is set.

Nutrition Information
- Calories: 372 calories
- Total Carbohydrate: 42 g
- Cholesterol: 98 mg
- Total Fat: 22 g
- Fiber: 2 g
- Protein: 5 g
- Sodium: 187 mg

Chocolate-Topped Strawberry Cheesecake

"Your dining table looks elegant because of this enticing and gorgeous dessert. It's a perfect blend of smooth strawberry cheesecake and brittle chocolate crust. Enjoy!"

Serving: 12 servings. | Prep: 35m | Ready in: 45m

Ingredients

- 1-1/4 cups chocolate graham cracker crumbs (about 9 whole crackers)
- 1/4 cup butter, melted
- 2 envelopes unflavored gelatin
- 1/2 cup cold water
- 16 oz. fresh or frozen unsweetened strawberries, thawed
- 2 packages (8 oz. each) fat-free cream cheese, cubed
- 1 cup fat-free cottage cheese
- Sugar substitute equivalent to 3/4 cup sugar
- 1 carton (8 oz.) frozen reduced-fat whipped topping, thawed, divided
- 1/2 cup chocolate ice cream topping
- 1 cup quartered fresh strawberries

Direction

- Set the oven and preheat at 350°F. Use cooking spray to coat the 9-inches springform pan. Mix butter and cracker crumbs and pour the mixture onto the bottom and 1-inch sides of the pan. Place the pan on a baking sheet and bake it inside the preheated oven for 10 minutes until set. Transfer on a wire rack to cool.

- Add gelatin in a small saucepan with cold water. Set aside for 1 minute. Cook and stir on low heat until the gelatin dissolves completely. Remove the mixture from the heat.
- Remove the hull from the strawberries if needed. Blend the strawberries in a food processor and transfer it into a bowl. Blend sugar substitute, cream cheese, and cottage cheese in a food processor until smooth. Add gelatin mixture gradually while the processor is running. Stir in pureed strawberries and process until well-blended. Pour the mixture into a big bowl. Add in 2 cups of whipped topping. Spread the mixture all over the crust. Cover and refrigerate for 2-3 hours until all set.
- Loosen the sides of the cheesecake using a knife and remove the rim. Top the cheesecake with the chocolate topping, the whipped topping, and the quartered strawberries before serving.

Nutrition Information
- Calories: 244 calories
- Total Carbohydrate: 29 g
- Cholesterol: 16 mg
- Total Fat: 8 g
- Fiber: 2 g

- Protein: 10 g
- Sodium: 464 mg

Chocolaty Almond Cheesecake

"With an extraordinary flavor, your guests will ask for more."
Serving: 12 servings. | Prep: 30m | Ready in: 30m

Ingredients

- 2 cups crushed vanilla wafers
- 1 cup finely chopped almonds, toasted
- 1/3 cup sugar
- 1/2 cup butter, melted
- FILLING:
- 1 envelope unflavored gelatin
- 1/2 cup milk
- 2 packages (8 oz. each) cream cheese, softened
- 1/2 cup sour cream
- 1/4 to 1/2 tsp. almond extract
- 1 package (11-1/2 oz.) milk chocolate chips, melted and cooled
- 1/2 cup heavy whipping cream, whipped
- Milk chocolate kisses, unblanched whole almonds and additional whipped cream

Direction

- Mix almonds, sugar and wafer crumbs. Add in butter. In a greased 9-in springform pan, press the mixture on bottom and 1 3/4 in. up sides. Cover and chill for 1 hour.

• Soften gelatin in the milk in a saucepan, let sit 5 minutes. Stir and cook over medium heat until gelatin is dissolved completely. Let cool for 6 minutes to room temperature.

• Mix sour cream, cream cheese and almond extract. Add in gelatin mixture and melted chocolate. Fold in the whipped cream and pour into the crust. Cover and refrigerate for 6 hours or overnight.

• Right before you serve, loosen from pan by running a knife around the edges. Take off pan's sides. Use almonds, more whipped cream, and chocolate kisses to garnish. Keep leftovers in fridge.

Coconut-White Chocolate Cheesecake

"Try not to overmix the batter to have the best result. My friends suggested that I should post this delicious recipe on a magazine."
Serving: 16 servings. | Prep: 40m | Ready in: 01h40m

Ingredients

- 1-1/2 cups graham cracker crumbs
- 6 tbsps. butter, melted
- 5 packages (8 oz. each) cream cheese, softened
- 1 cup sugar
- 1-1/2 cups white baking chips, melted and cooled
- 3/4 cup coconut milk
- 2 tsps. coconut extract
- 1 tsp. vanilla extract
- 4 large eggs, lightly beaten
- 3/4 cup sweetened shredded coconut, toasted, divided

Direction

- Set the oven to 325°F for preheating. Place the greased springform pan (about 9-inches in size and 3-inches deep) on a double thickness of heavy-duty foil (about 18-inches square). Secure the foil tightly around the pan.

- Mix butter and cracker crumbs in a small bowl. Pour it at the bottom of the greased pan.
- Whisk sugar and cream cheese in a big bowl until smooth. Stir in extracts, coconut milk, and cooled chips. Beat in eggs and mix at low speed until well-blended. Add a half cup of coconut. Drizzle mixture all over the crust. Place the pan in a big baking pan with an inch hot water.
- Let it bake inside the preheated oven for 60-70 minutes until its top looks dull and the center is fixed. Remove the pan from the water bath and place it in a wire rack. Cool for 10 minutes. Use a knife to loosen the sides of the pan. Remove the foil. Let it cool for 60 more minutes. Cover and refrigerate the cheesecake overnight.
- Remove the rim from the pan. Top the cheesecake with coconut, and then serve.

Nutrition Information
- Calories: 517 calories
- Total Carbohydrate: 32 g
- Cholesterol: 144 mg
- Total Fat: 40 g
- Fiber: 1 g
- Protein: 9 g
- Sodium: 332 mg

Coffee Lover's Mini Cheesecakes

""All my love ones knows how much I love cheesecake. They always asked me to prepare this since they know I have tested many recipes. And I was getting tired with the normal cherry or chocolate. Then I ended with this idea; mocha cheesecake! After many attempts, finally made this recipe. Really great, even if I do say myself.""
Serving: 2 dozen. | Prep: 30m | Ready in: 50m

Ingredients

- 30 chocolate wafers, finely crushed (about 1-2/3 cups crumbs)
- 1/4 cup sugar
- 2 tbsps. butter, melted
- 2 tbsps. brewed espresso
- FILLING:
- 8 oz. semisweet chocolate
- 2 tbsps. brewed espresso
- 3 packages (8 oz. each) cream cheese, softened
- 1 can (14 oz.) sweetened condensed milk
- 4 large eggs, room temperature and lightly beaten
- 2 cups frozen whipped topping, thawed
- 24 chocolate-covered coffee beans
- Baking cocoa, optional

Direction

- Prepare the oven by preheating to 325°F. Use foil liners to line 24 muffin cups. Combine sugar and wafer crumbs; mix in espresso and butter. Then push down by tablespoonfuls onto bottoms of liners. To make filling, place chocolate in a microwave to melt; mix in espresso until combined. Whip cream cheese in a large bowl until turns smooth; gently mix in condensed milk until well combined. Add chocolate mixture into cream cheese mixture until mixed well. Put in eggs; beat just until combined. Put 1/4 cup cheesecake batter to fill prepared cups. Place in the preheated oven and bake for 17-20 minutes until centers are almost set. Let cool in pans for 10 minutes before taking to wire racks to fully cool. Place in the refrigerator overnight, covering when fully cooled. To serve, place whipped topping and chocolate-covered coffee beans on top; and sprinkle with baking cocoa if desired.

Nutrition Information
- Calories: 308 calories
- Total Carbohydrate: 25 g
- Cholesterol: 70 mg
- Total Fat: 19 g
- Fiber: 1 g
- Protein: 6 g
- Sodium: 181 mg

Contest-Winning White Chocolate Cheesecake

""This chocolate cheesecake recipe is my best favorite! Shared by a friend a couple years ago and I've created lots of these yummy cakes over the years. They bring me flattery all the time.""
Serving: 12 servings. | Prep: 40m | Ready in: 01h25m

Ingredients
- 7 whole cinnamon graham crackers, crushed
- 1/4 cup sugar
- 1/3 cup butter, melted
- FILLING:
- 4 packages (8 oz. each) cream cheese, softened
- 1/2 cup plus 2 tbsps. sugar
- 1 tbsp. all-purpose flour
- 1 tsp. vanilla extract
- 4 large eggs, lightly beaten
- 2 large egg yolks, lightly beaten
- 8 oz. white baking chocolate, melted and cooled
- STRAWBERRY SAUCE:
- 1/2 cup sugar
- 2 tbsps. cornstarch
- 1/2 cup water
- 1-1/2 cups chopped fresh strawberries
- Red food coloring, optional
- Melted white chocolate

Direction

- Mix in a small bowl the sugar and cracker crumbs; mix in butter. Push down onto the bottom and 1-inch up the sides of a greased 10-inch springform pan.
- Whisk vanilla, flour, sugar and cream cheese in a large bowl until well combined. Put in yolks and eggs; whisk on low speed just until blended. Mix in white chocolate. Place over crust. Put the pan on a baking sheet.
- Put in the oven and bake for 45-50 minutes at 350°F or until middle is just set. Cool for 10 minutes on a wire rack. Gently run a knife around the edge of the pan to loosen; cool for 1 more hour. Place in the refrigerator for overnight.
- To make sauce, mix in a large saucepan the water, cornstarch and sugar until it turns smooth. Put in strawberries. Make it boil; stir and cook until thickened. Separate from heat; mix in a few drops of food coloring if wished. Let it cool.
- Put strawberry sauce over the top of cheesecake then spread; drizzle with melted white chocolate. Keep leftovers in the refrigerator.

Nutrition Information

- Calories: 572 calories
- Total Carbohydrate: 46 g
- Cholesterol: 205 mg
- Total Fat: 41 g
- Fiber: 1 g

- Protein: 10 g
- Sodium: 348 mg

Cranberry Mocha Cheesecake

""Prepare this delicious dessert for quite a few occasions, and a tremendous hit all the time. Perfect finale with cranberries to a dinner for holiday.""
Serving: 14 servings. | Prep: 30m | Ready in: 01h20m

Ingredients

- 1 package (9 oz.) chocolate wafer cookies, crushed
- 1/3 cup butter, melted
- FILLING:
- 4 packages (8 oz. each) cream cheese, softened
- 1-1/3 cups sugar
- 1 tbsp. all-purpose flour
- 4 large eggs
- 2 tbsps. instant coffee granules
- 1 tbsp. hot water
- 1/4 cup heavy whipping cream
- 1-1/2 tsps. ground cinnamon
- TOPPING:
- 1 tbsp. cornstarch
- 1 can (14 oz.) whole-berry cranberry sauce
- 3/4 cup heavy whipping cream
- 1/2 tsp. vanilla extract
- 2 tbsps. confectioners' sugar

Direction

- Mix butter and cookie crumbs; press onto the bottom and about 2-inch up the sides of a 9-inch springform pan that was greased; reserve. Beat cream cheese in a large bowl until it turns smooth. Combine the flour and sugar; then add to cream cheese and blend well. Put in eggs; whisk on low speed just until mixed.
- Dissolve coffee in the water in a small bowl; mix in cinnamon and cream. Mix into the cream cheese mixture just until combined. Place over crust. Put pan on a baking sheet.
- Bake in the oven for 50-55 minutes at 350°F or until middle is nearly set. Place on a wire rack and cool for 10 minutes. Cautiously run a knife around the edge of the pan to loosen; cool for 1 more hour.
- Put the cranberry sauce and cornstarch in a large saucepan and make it boil. Stir and cook for 2 minutes or until thickened. Let it cool.
- Whisk vanilla and cream in a small bowl until it forms soft peaks. Gently add in confectioner's sugar, whisking until it forms stiff peaks. Then spread over the cheesecake. Place in the refrigerator for 20 minutes or until set.
- Gently spread 1 cup of cranberry mixture to within 1-inch of the edge; put the remaining cranberry mixture in the refrigerator, covered. Keep cheesecake in the refrigerator overnight. Then serve with the remaining cranberry mixture.

Nutrition Information

- Calories: 384 calories
- Total Carbohydrate: 48 g
- Cholesterol: 114 mg
- Total Fat: 20 g
- Fiber: 1 g
- Protein: 5 g
- Sodium: 230 mg

Cranberry Orange Cheesecake

""I can't attend any Christmas get together without this amazing dessert in tow. The mix of orange, chocolate and cranberries is a winner.""
Serving: 12 servings. | Prep: 45m | Ready in: 01h45m

Ingredients
- 1 cup finely chopped pecans
- 2/3 cup chocolate wafer crumbs
- 1/4 cup butter, melted
- 3 tbsps. brown sugar
- 2 packages (8 oz. each) cream cheese, softened
- 2 cartons (8 oz. each) mascarpone cheese
- 1-1/4 cups sugar
- 2 tbsps. cornstarch
- 2 tsps. orange juice
- 1 tsp. orange extract
- 4 large eggs, lightly beaten
- 3/4 cup whole-berry cranberry sauce
- 1/4 cup dried cranberries
- 1 tbsp. water
- 1/4 cup chocolate ice cream topping, warmed

Direction

- Put a 9-inch springform pan, greased, on a double thickness of heavy-duty foil (about 18in. Squares).Tightly wrap foil around pan.

- Mix brown sugar, butter, wafer crumbs and pecans. Then press onto the bottom and 1-inch up the sides of prepared pan. Put on a baking sheet. Put in the oven and bake for 8-10 minutes at 325°F or until lightly browned. Put on a wire rack to cool. Beat extract, orange juice, cornstarch, sugar and cheeses in a large bowl until smooth. Put in eggs; whisk on low speed just until mixed. Put half of the batter over crust.
- In a food processor, put the water, cranberries and cranberry sauce; then cover and blend until mixed. Carefully spread over batter in pan; put remaining batter on top.
- Put springform pan in a large baking pan; put in 1-inch of hot water to large pan. Then bake for 60-70 minutes at 325°F or until middle is almost set and top looks dull.
- Take pan from water bath. Put on a wire rack to cool for 10 minutes. Gently run a knife around edge of pan to loosen; cool for 1 more hour. Keep in the refrigerator for overnight. Drizzle with chocolate topping just before serving.

Nutrition Information
- Calories: 599 calories
- Total Carbohydrate: 45 g
- Cholesterol: 169 mg
- Total Fat: 44 g
- Fiber: 2 g
- Protein: 9 g

- Sodium: 229 mg

Cranberry White Chocolate Chunk Cheesecake

"This New York-inspired cheesecake is a perfect dessert to serve on a gathering. It has a flavor of cranberries, bits of white chocolate and a pinch of yuletide red."
Serving: 16 servings. | Prep: 30m | Ready in: 01h30m

Ingredients
- 15 Oreo cookies, finely crushed (about 1-1/2 cups)
- 1/3 cup butter, melted
- CHEESECAKE:
- 5 packages (8 oz. each) cream cheese, softened
- 1-1/2 cups sugar
- 1 tbsp. cranberry juice or 2% milk
- 1 tbsp. vanilla extract
- 3 large eggs, lightly beaten
- 12 oz. white baking chocolate, cut into 1/2-in. pieces
- 1 cup dried cranberries

Direction
- Set the oven to 325°F for preheating. Place the greased 10-inches springform pan over an 18-inch double thick and heavy-duty square shaped foil. Fold the foil tightly around the pan.
- Whisk melted butter and crushed cookies in a small bowl. Spread it into the bottom of the greased pan.
- Mix sugar and cream cheese in a big bowl until smooth. Stir in vanilla and cranberry juice. Beat in eggs

and whisk at low speed just until combined. Whisk in cranberries and white chocolate. Pour the mixture into the pan with crust. Place the pan in a big baking pan with an inch of hot water.
- Let it bake inside the preheated oven for 60-70 minutes until the top appears dull and its center is set. Transfer the pan on a wire rack and cool for 10 minutes. Use a knife to loosen the sides of the pan. Remove the foil and let it cool for 60 more minutes. Cover and refrigerate overnight. Remove the rim from the pan. Serve.

Nutrition Information
- Calories: 545 calories
- Total Carbohydrate: 50 g
- Cholesterol: 123 mg
- Total Fat: 37 g
- Fiber: 1 g
- Protein: 7 g
- Sodium: 362 mg

Deluxe Chip Cheesecake

"We love cheesecake. We prepared this delicious dessert once as a treat for travelling basket. However, it looks so amazing and we decide to give a different treat."

Serving: 12-14 servings. | Prep: 25m | Ready in: 01h20m

Ingredients
- 1-1/2 cups crushed vanilla wafers (about 45 wafers)
- 1/2 cup confectioners' sugar
- 1/4 cup baking cocoa
- 1/3 cup butter, melted
- FILLING:
- 3 packages (8 oz. each) cream cheese, softened
- 3/4 cup sugar
- 1/3 cup sour cream
- 3 tbsps. all-purpose flour
- 1 tsp. vanilla extract
- 1/4 tsp. salt
- 3 eggs, lightly beaten
- 1 cup butterscotch chips, melted
- 1 cup (6 oz.) semisweet chocolate chips, melted
- 1 cup white baking chips
- TOPPING:
- 1 tbsp. each butterscotch, semisweet chocolate and vanilla or white chips
- 1-1/2 tsps. shortening

Direction

• Mix in a big bowl the cocoa, confectioner's sugar, butter and wafer crumbs. Press onto the bottom and 1-1/2 inch up the sides of the greased 9-in. springform pan. Place inside the oven and bake for 7-9 minutes or until set at 350 degrees. Transfer to a wire rack to cool.

• Beat until smooth the sugar and cream cheese in a big bowl. Mix flour, vanilla, salt and sour cream. Add in eggs and beat on low speed just until mixed. Take out 1-1/2 cups batter to a bowl; mix in butterscotch chips.

• Pour over the crust. Put chocolate chips to another 1-1/2 cups batter and gently spoon onto the butterscotch layer. Mix vanilla chips into the remaining batter and spoon onto the chocolate layer.

• Place inside the oven and bake until nearly set or for 55-60 minutes at 350 degrees. Transfer on a wire rack to cool for 10 minutes. Gently use a knife to run around the edge of a pan to loosen. Let it cool for 1 hour.

• In a 3 small microwaveable bowls, put 1/2 tsp. shortening and each flavor of chips for the topping. Place in a microwave on high for 25 seconds and then stir. Warm in 10 to 20 second intervals, stirring until smooth. Drizzle over cheesecake. Refrigerate for at least 3 hours. Take away sides of the pan. Place leftovers in the refrigerator.

Nutrition Information

• Calories: 479 calories
• Total Carbohydrate: 55 g

- Cholesterol: 84 mg
- Total Fat: 28 g
- Fiber: 1 g
- Protein: 6 g
- Sodium: 217 mg

Double Chip Cheesecake Bars

"Cooking is my passion and I also create my own recipes. This dessert is one of my own creations."
Serving: 3 dozen. | Prep: 15m | Ready in: 55m

Ingredients

- 2 cups all-purpose flour
- 1/2 cup confectioners' sugar
- 1 cup cold butter, cubed
- FILLING:
- 2 packages (8 oz. each) cream cheese, softened
- 1/2 cup packed brown sugar
- 2 eggs
- 1 tsp. almond extract
- 1 cup (6 oz.) semisweet chocolate chips, divided
- 1/2 cup butterscotch chips
- 1/2 cup chopped walnuts

Direction

- Mix confectioner's sugar and flour in a big bowl. Cut in butter until the mixture looks like coarse crumbs. Press into 13 inches x 9 inches ungreased baking pan. Bake for 18-22 minutes or until it becomes lightly browned at 350 degrees.

- In the meantime, beat brown sugar and cream cheese until smooth in big bowl. Stir in eggs and extract. Mix in walnuts, butterscotch chips and 1/2 cup chocolate chips. Spread over the crust. Sprinkle with leftover chocolate chips.

• Place inside the oven and bake for 20-25 minutes or until center is j nearly set. Let it cool fully on a wire rack prior to slicing. Refrigerate leftovers

Nutrition Information

- Calories: 166 calories
- Total Carbohydrate: 15 g
- Cholesterol: 33 mg
- Total Fat: 11 g
- Fiber: 1 g
- Protein: 2 g
- Sodium: 78 mg

Double Chocolate Almond Cheesecake

""Simple to prepare cheesecake; but it's surely won't last a day! This recipe is a from a colleague.""
Serving: 12-16 servings. | Prep: 25m | Ready in: 01h15m

Ingredients
- CRUST:
- 1 package (9 oz.) chocolate wafer cookies, crushed (about 2 cups)
- 1/4 cup sugar
- 1/4 tsp. ground cinnamon
- 1/4 cup butter, melted
- FILLING:
- 2 packages (8 oz. each) cream cheese, softened
- 1 cup sugar
- 1 cup sour cream
- 8 oz. semisweet chocolate, melted and cooled
- 1/2 tsp. almond extract
- 2 large eggs, lightly beaten
- TOPPING:
- 1 cup sour cream
- 1/4 tsp. baking cocoa
- 2 tbsps. sugar
- 1/2 tsp. almond extract
- Sliced almonds, toasted, optional

Direction

- Mix in a small bowl the crust ingredients; set aside 2 tbsps. for decorate. Push remaining crumbs equally onto the bottom and 2 inch up the sides of a 9-inch springform pan. Let chill. To make filling, whisk in a large bowl the sugar and cream cheese until turns smooth. Mix in the extract, chocolate, and sour cream. Put in eggs; whisk on low speed just until mixed. Place into crust. Put the pan on a baking sheet. Place in the oven and bake for 40 minutes at 350°F (filling will not be set). Take from the oven and allow to stand for 5 minutes. In the meantime, mix topping ingredients. Cautiously spread over filling. Dust with set aside crumbs. Bake for 10 more minutes. Then place on a wire rack and cool for 10 minutes. Use a knife and gently run around edge of pan to loosen; let cool for 1 more hour. Place in the refrigerator for overnight. Decorate with sliced, toasted almonds if want.

Nutrition Information

- Calories: 315 calories
- Total Carbohydrate: 31 g
- Cholesterol: 78 mg
- Total Fat: 19 g
- Fiber: 1 g
- Protein: 4 g
- Sodium: 215 mg

Double Chocolate Espresso Cheesecake

"Coffee and chocolate are really a perfect combination! I love how their combination adds a delicious flavor into this creamy cheesecake."
Serving: 16 servings. | Prep: 35m | Ready in: 01h35m

Ingredients
- 1-1/2 cups crushed vanilla wafers (about 45)
- 1/4 cup butter, melted
- 2 tbsps. sugar
- 1/4 tsp. instant espresso powder
- FILLING:
- 4 packages (8 oz. each) cream cheese, softened
- 1-1/2 cups sugar
- 1 cup sour cream
- 1 cup 60% cacao bittersweet chocolate baking chips, melted
- 1/2 cup baking cocoa
- 1/4 cup half-and-half cream
- 1 tbsp. all-purpose flour
- 5 large eggs, lightly beaten
- 1-1/2 tsps. instant espresso powder
- 1 tsp. vanilla extract
- TOPPING:
- 1 cup coffee liqueur
- 1 tbsp. half-and-half cream

- 1 cup heavy whipping cream
- 2 tbsps. confectioners' sugar
- 1/2 cup 60% cacao bittersweet chocolate baking chips, chopped
- 16 chocolate-covered coffee beans

Direction

- Set the greased 9-inches springform pan over an 18-inches square double thickness of heavy-duty foil. Wrap the foil tightly around the pan.
- Mix butter, espresso powder, wafer crumbs, and sugar in a big bowl. Pour the mixture at the bottom and an inch up sides of the prepared pan.
- Whisk cocoa, sour cream, flour, melted chocolate, cream, cream cheese, and sugar in a big bowl until smooth. Add the eggs and whisk at low speed just until blended. Mix in vanilla and espresso powder. Pour the mixture into the crust. Place the pan in a big baking pan with an inch of hot water inside.
- Set the oven to 350°F and bake for 60-70 minutes until the top looks dull and the center is fixed. Transfer the pan from the water bath into the wire rack. Cool for 10 minutes. Loosen the edges of the pan using a sharp knife and let it cool for 60 more minutes. Refrigerate the cheesecake whole night. Remove the rim from the pan.
- Mix half-and-half and liqueur in a small saucepan and bring the mixture to boil. Heat it until the liquid gets reduced to half. Whisk whipping cream in a big bowl

until thick. Stir in confectioners' sugar and beat until it forms stiff peaks.
- Spread the coffee syrup on top of the cheesecake and garnish it with the whipped cream, coffee beans, and chocolate.

Nutrition Information
- Calories: 610 calories
- Total Carbohydrate: 52 g
- Cholesterol: 170 mg
- Total Fat: 40 g
- Fiber: 2 g
- Protein: 9 g
- Sodium: 259 mg

Dressed-Up Cheesecake

"Make some twists to your plain cheesecake by adding some simple ingredients. Before serving, garnish it with some swirls of chocolate syrup so that it looks like it was prepared by a real master baker." Serving: 6-8 servings. | Prep: 5m | Ready in: 5m

Ingredients
- 1/2 cup milk chocolate toffee bits
- 1/4 cup caramel ice cream topping
- 1 frozen New York-style cheesecake (30 oz.), thawed
- Chocolate syrup

Direction
- Mix caramel toppings and toffee bits in a small bowl; put on cheesecake and spread. Put some chocolate syrup on the dessert plate before serving, together with a slice of your new-look cheesecake.

Nutrition Information
- Calories: 447 calories
- Total Carbohydrate: 42 g
- Cholesterol: 71 mg
- Total Fat: 29 g
- Fiber: 1 g
- Protein: 6 g
- Sodium: 323 mg

Dulce De Leche Cheesecake

"It's one of the best Dulce de Leche Cheesecake with tasty, creamy, dreamy flavor."
Serving: 12 servings | Prep: 15m | Ready in: 6h10m

Ingredients

- 3 pkg. (8 oz. each) PHILADELPHIA Cream Cheese , softened
- 1/2 cup sugar , divided
- 1 cup dulce de leche (sweetened milk caramel)
- 1/2 cup BREAKSTONE'S or KNUDSEN Sour Cream
- 3 egg s
- 1 cup honey-flavored multi-grain cereal flakes with oat clusters
- 1/2 cup thawed COOL WHIP Whipped Topping

Direction

- 1. In a big bowl, mix 1/4 cup sugar and cream cheese using a mixer until blended. Mix in thoroughly sour cream and dulce de leche. One at a time, add in eggs, combine on low speed after each addition until blended. Turn the mixture into 9" greased with cooking spray springform pan.

- 2. Bake until the middle is mostly set, or for 50-55 minutes. To loosen cake, run knife around rim of pan. Cool before removing rim. Chill cheesecake in fridge for 4 hours.
- 3. At the same time, in moderate-size saucepan, cook leftover sugar on medium heat for 4 minutes, or until melted and has golden brown color. Take out of heat. Stir in cereal and place on baking sheet by spreading into thin layer. Let it cool.
- 4. Before serving, put on top of the cheesecake the cereal mixture and cool whip.

Nutrition Information
- Calories: 360
- Total Carbohydrate: 29 g
- Cholesterol: 135 mg
- Total Fat: 24 g
- Fiber: 0 g
- Protein: 7 g
- Sodium: 280 mg
- Sugar: 23 g
- Saturated Fat: 15 g

Easy Cheesecake Pie

""A simply yet luscious cheesecake recipe. It normally takes about 5 minutes (10 minutes tops) to make this up.""
Serving: 8

Ingredients

- 1 (12 oz.) container frozen whipped topping, thawed
- 1/3 cup white sugar
- 1 tsp. vanilla extract
- 1 (8 oz.) package cream cheese
- 1 (9 inch) pie shell, baked

Direction

- Remove cream cheese out of package, and put in microwave for 30 seconds to soften. Combine sugar, vanilla, whipped topping and cream cheese in a large bowl until turns smooth.
- Place filling into pie crust. Place in the refrigerator for 3 hours.

Nutrition Information

- Calories: 384 calories;
- Total Carbohydrate: 29.5 g
- Cholesterol: 31 mg
- Total Fat: 28.2 g

- Protein: 4.1 g
- Sodium: 215 mg

Easy Chocolate Cherry Cheesecups

"This yummy cheesecake is so good with a made easy recipe. Cheesecake with a delightful cherry flavor!"
Serving: 2 dozen. | Prep: 20m | Ready in: 40m

Ingredients
- 24 vanilla wafers

- 2 packages (8 oz. each) cream cheese, softened
- 1 cup sour cream
- 1-1/4 cups sugar
- 1/2 cup baking cocoa
- 3 large eggs
- 1/2 to 1 tsp. almond extract
- 1 tsp. vanilla extract
- Whipped topping
- Cherry pie filling or maraschino cherries

Direction
- In muffin cups lined with paper, put vanilla wafers with flat side down. Set aside. Mix sour cream, sugar and cream cheese in a bowl until smooth. Blend in eggs, cocoa and extract.
- Fill the muffin cups with the mixture three-fourths full. Bake for 20-25 minutes at 325 degrees until tops are puffy. Let cool on wire rack. Place cover and chill until serving. Top with whipped topping and cherries or cherry pie filling.

Nutrition Information
- Calories: 126 calories
- Total Carbohydrate: 15 g
- Cholesterol: 44 mg
- Total Fat: 6 g
- Fiber: 0 g
- Protein: 2 g
- Sodium: 53 mg

Fabulous Fudge Cheesecake

"Make this fudgy cheesecake the favorite of your guests at your party."
Serving: 10-12 servings. | Prep: 10m | Ready in: 50m

Ingredients

- 1 cup crushed vanilla wafers (about 30 wafers)
- 1/2 cup confectioners' sugar
- 1/3 cup baking cocoa
- 1/3 cup butter, melted
- FILLING:
- 3 packages (8 oz. each) cream cheese, softened
- 2 cups (12 oz.) semisweet chocolate chips, melted and cooled
- 1 can (14 oz.) sweetened condensed milk
- 2 tsps. vanilla extract
- 4 eggs

Direction

- Combine sugar, cocoa, and wafer crumbs in a bowl. Add butter. In a greased 9-inch springform pan, press the mixture on bottom and set aside.

- Beat cream cheese in another bowl until smooth. Slowly add in chocolate. Beat in eggs on low speed until just mixed. Slowly stir in vanilla and milk. Put mixture on crust. Place springform pan on a baking sheet.

- Bake for 40-45 minutes or until middle is nearly set at 325 degrees. Let cool for 10 minutes on wire rack. Loosen edges with knife, let cool for another hour. Chill overnight. Take off the sides of the pan. Chill leftovers.

Nutrition Information
- Calories: 446 calories
- Total Carbohydrate: 50 g
- Cholesterol: 117 mg
- Total Fat: 26 g
- Fiber: 2 g
- Protein: 8 g
- Sodium: 204 mg

Favorite Lemon Cheesecake

"This mouthwatering light lemon mini dessert matches the flavor of the chocolate crush which is made from home "A good friend gave this recipe and it's perfect for all occasions, whether dinners, birthdays or anniversaries.""

Serving: 2-4 servings. | Prep: 15m | Ready in: 60m

Ingredients

- 1/2 cup crushed chocolate wafers
- 2 tbsps. butter, melted
- 1 package (8 oz.) cream cheese, softened
- 1/2 cup sugar
- 1/2 cup sour cream
- 2 tbsps. lemon juice
- 1 tbsp. all-purpose flour
- 1 tsp. grated lemon peel
- 1/2 tsp. vanilla extract
- 1 egg, lightly beaten

Direction

- Mix butter and wafer crumbs in a small bowl. Press down onto the bottom of a 6 inches springform pan. Put pan on a baking sheet. Place in an oven and bake for 7-8 minutes at 350 degrees. Transfer on a wire rack to cool.

- Beat sugar and cream cheese in a big bowl. Blend in lemon juice, sour cream, lemon peel, flour and vanilla. Add egg; beat egg on low speed just until incorporated. Pour over crust.
- Transfer pan on a baking sheet. Place in an oven and bake for 35-40 minutes or until center is nearly set for. Cook on a wire rack and cool for 10 minutes. Gently run a knife around the edge of the pan to loosen; cool for 1 more hour.
- Store in the refrigerator for 8 hours or overnight. Take away sides of the pan. Put the leftovers in the refrigerator.

Festive Holiday Cheesecake

"In the search with the best Christmas cheesecake? This cheesecake is topped with fully loaded candy toppings."

Serving: 16 servings. | Prep: 30m | Ready in: 02h00m

Ingredients

- 1-1/2 cups graham cracker crumbs
- 1/2 cup pecans, toasted and finely chopped
- 2 tbsps. light brown sugar
- 6 tbsps. butter, melted
- FILLING:
- 4 packages (8 oz. each) cream cheese, softened
- 1 cup sugar
- 3 tsps. vanilla extract
- 4 eggs, lightly beaten
- 1 cup (6 oz.) miniature semisweet chocolate chips
- TOPPING:
- 2 cups (16 oz.) sour cream
- 1/4 cup sugar
- Assorted candies

Direction

- Securely wrap ungreased 9-inch sized springform pan using around 18-inch square heavy-duty foil.
- Mix ground crackers, brown sugar, pecans and butter in a small bowl. Spread it on the bottom of the

prepared pan about 1 to 1.5-inch-thick, put on a baking sheet and bake for 5 minutes at 350 °F. Place over a cooling wire rack.

- Combine cream cheese, vanilla and sugar in a big bowl and beat until smooth. Add eggs while beating on low speed just till combined and then fold in chocolate chips. Transfer the mixture to the prepared crust and place the pan over a larger baking pan to add 1-inch hot water.
- Bake it for around 1 to 1.5 hours at 350°F or until the center is firm and top part looks dull. On a small bowl, blend sugar and sour cream until smooth and spread all over hot cheesecake to cover. Bring it back to bake for another 5 minutes or until top portion appears to be firm.
- Transfer springform pan from water bath. Cool the cheesecake on a wire rack for about 10 minutes and loosen the edge of the pan by inserting a knife then allow to cool for an hour. Place inside the refrigerator overnight. Lift cheesecake from the can and decorate with candies.

Festive White Chocolate Cheesecake

"This cheesecake has a buttery crust, smooth white chocolate filling and delicious cranberry-raspberry sauce that tastes so evenly. It looks more elegant if you top it with berries and whipped cream. This recipe is surely a masterpiece that will undoubtedly win raves."
Serving: 12 servings. | Prep: 30m | Ready in: 01h05m

Ingredients
- 2 cups crushed shortbread cookies
- 1/4 cup butter, melted
- FILLING:
- 2 packages (8 oz. each) cream cheese, softened
- 1 cup white baking chips
- 2/3 cup sour cream
- 3/4 cup sugar
- 1 tbsp. grated orange zest
- 1 tsp. vanilla extract
- 3 large eggs, lightly beaten
- SAUCE:
- 1 cup whole-berry cranberry sauce
- 1/2 cup seedless raspberry jam
- 1/2 tsp. grated orange zest
- TOPPING:
- 2 cups heavy whipping cream
- 1/4 cup confectioners' sugar

Direction

- Mix butter and cookie crumbs in a small bowl. Drop the mixture into the bottom of a 9-inches springform pan that is greased. Set the mixture aside.
- Whisk chips, orange zest, vanilla, sour cream, cream cheese, and sugar in a big bowl until smooth. Stir in eggs and whisk at low speed until well-blended. Pour the mixture on the crust. Transfer the pan over the baking sheet.
- Let it bake inside the oven at 350°F for 35 to 40 minutes until the middle of the cake is almost fixed. Transfer it onto a wire rack and let it cool for 10 minutes. Use a knife to loosen the edges of the cake. Let it cool for 1 more hour before storing it inside the refrigerator.
- Mix all the sauce ingredients in a small saucepan. Allow it to cook over medium heat, stirring often until well-blended. Set aside to cool.
- Remove the cake from the springform pan. Pour the sauce over the cheesecake to within 1-inch from its edges. Whisk confectioners' sugar and cream in a small bowl until it forms stiff peaks. Style it up on top of the sauce, and then serve. Refrigerate any leftovers.

Nutrition Information

- Calories: 738 calories
- Total Carbohydrate: 68 g
- Cholesterol: 177 mg
- Total Fat: 49 g

- Fiber: 1 g
- Protein: 9 g
- Sodium: 364 mg

Frosted Chocolate Chip Cheesecake

""Described as a 'divine' for this yummy dessert, suitably prepared a day in advance. I melt 3/4 cup of chocolate chips when candy bar is not available on hand to use in the frosting. And you can use whipped cream instead of whipped topping.""
Serving: 12 servings. | Prep: 40m | Ready in: 01h35m

Ingredients

- 2 cups chocolate wafer crumbs
- 6 tbsps. butter, melted
- FILLING:
- 3 packages (8 oz. each) cream cheese, softened
- 1 cup sugar
- 1 tsp. vanilla extract
- 3 eggs, lightly beaten
- 1 cup (6 oz.) miniature semisweet chocolate chips
- 1 milk chocolate candy bar (4 oz.), chopped
- 2 cups whipped topping
- 1/4 cup sliced almonds, toasted

Direction

- Mix in a small bowl the butter and wafer crumbs. Then press onto the bottom and 1-1/2-inch up the sides of a 9-inch springform pan that is greased. Let chill for 15 minutes or until set. Beat vanilla, sugar and cream cheese in a large bowl until smooth. Put in eggs; whisk on low speed just until mixed. Mix in chocolate chips. Place into crust. Put the pan on a baking sheet. Place in the oven and bake for 55-60 minutes at 325°F or until middle is just set. Put on a wire rack to cool for 10 minutes. Gently run a knife around edge of pan to loosen; cool for1 more hour. Refrigerate overnight, covered. To make frosting, melt candy bar in a microwave-safe bowl; stir until turn smooth. Cool to room temperature. Gently mix in whipped topping. Then frost top of cheesecake; decorate with almonds. Keep leftovers in the refrigerator.

Nutrition Information
- Calories: 442 calories
- Total Carbohydrate: 48 g
- Cholesterol: 92 mg
- Total Fat: 26 g
- Fiber: 2 g
- Protein: 6 g
- Sodium: 247 mg

Frosty Summer Dessert

Serving: 4 servings. | Prep: 15m | Ready in: 15m

Ingredients

- 3/4 cup crushed chocolate wafers
- 3 tbsps. butter
- 4 oz. cream cheese, softened
- 3/4 cup thawed apple-raspberry juice concentrate
- 1 tbsp. confectioners' sugar
- 1 cup whipped topping

Direction

- Mix in a small bowl the butter and wafer crumbs. The press onto the bottom of a 6-inch springform pan coated with cooking spray; reserve.
- Beat confectioner's sugar, juice concentrate and cream cheese in a small bowl. Add in whipped topping and fold. Put over crust. Freeze for 4 hours or until firm, covered. Take out from the freezer 5-10 minutes prior to serving.

Nutrition Information

- Calories: 328 calories
- Total Carbohydrate: 43 g
- Cholesterol: 35 mg

- Total Fat: 15 g
- Fiber: 1 g
- Protein: 6 g
- Sodium: 297 mg

Frozen Brownie Cheesecake

""This cheesecake had a vanilla ice cream in it the first time we tasted it at a friend's. I prepared it the way it was ever since when I chose to make it and I could only find chocolate ice cream! Children love this for their birthdays since it mixes ice cream and cake.""
Serving: 12-16 servings. | Prep: 30m | Ready in: 55m

Ingredients
- CRUST:
- 3/4 cup sugar
- 1/2 cup butter, softened
- 2 large eggs
- 1/2 cup all-purpose flour
- 1/2 cup baking cocoa
- 1/2 tsp. baking powder
- 1/2 tsp. salt
- FILLING:
- 1 package (8 oz.) cream cheese, softened
- 1/4 cup light corn syrup
- 1 quart chocolate ice cream, softenend
- 1 jar (18 oz.) hot fudge sauce

Direction
- Beat butter and cream sugar in a large bowl. Put in eggs. Mix dry ingredients; then put into cream mixture. Tap into the bottom of a 9-inch springform pan. Place

in the oven and bake for 25-30 minutes at 350°F. Cool. In the meantime, to make filling, mix corn syrup and cream cheese in a bowl. Mix in ice cream. Scoop half of the filling over crust; put half of the fudge sauce on t op. Then cover with remaining filling. Freeze for 4 hours or overnight, covered. Once ready to serve, pipe remaining fudge sauce in parallel strips over top of cake. Drag a knife across strips in opposite direction.

Nutrition Information
- Calories: 359 calories
- Total Carbohydrate: 47 g
- Cholesterol: 69 mg
- Total Fat: 17 g
- Fiber: 2 g
- Protein: 6 g
- Sodium: 266 mg

Frozen Cheesecake Bites

"One bite of this cheesecake satisfies your cravings, but you can ask for more."
Serving: 5-1/2 dozen. | Prep: 60m | Ready in: 01h40m

Ingredients

- 3 packages (8 oz. each) cream cheese, softened
- 1-1/4 cups sugar, divided
- 1-1/2 tsps. vanilla extract
- 1/2 tsp. salt
- 4 eggs, lightly beaten
- 9 oz. semisweet chocolate, chopped
- 3/4 cup heavy whipping cream
- 1/2 cup graham cracker crumbs
- 1/2 cup milk chocolate English toffee bits

Direction

- In a 9-inch springform pan, line the base with parchment paper. Spray the paper and sides with cooking spray and set aside. Mix cream cheese, vanilla, 1 cup sugar, and salt in a big bowl until smooth. Beat in eggs on low speed until just blended, and transfer into the pan.

- Put the pan in a baking sheet and bake for 40-45 minutes at 325 degrees or until middle is nearly set. Let cool for 10 minutes on a wire rack. Loosen edges carefully with a knife and let cool for another 1 hour. Chill, covered, in freezer overnight.

• Take out from freezer and let sit until it can be handled easily, 30 minutes. Melt chocolate and cream over low heat in a saucepan. Stir until mixed thoroughly. Take off heat and pour into a big bowl. Cover and chill until it has spreading texture, occasionally stir.

• Mix cracker crumbs and left sugar in a bowl. Use a melon baller to scoop 1-in. balls from cheesecake and put on baking sheets lined with parchment paper. Put 1 heaping tsp. of chocolate mixture on each ball. Divide balls and sprinkle half with crumb mixture and the other half with toffee bits. Chill in freezer until firm, 2 hours.

Nutrition Information
- Calories: 55 calories
- Total Carbohydrate: 6 g
- Cholesterol: 21 mg
- Total Fat: 3 g
- Fiber: 0 g
- Protein: 1 g
- Sodium: 47 mg

Frozen Chocolate Cheesecake Tart

""I first created this tempting dessert for some dinner visitors. And everyone was overwhelmed by its looks and rich taste. My hubby said that it was the best dessert he had ever have in his entire life.""
Serving: 12 servings. | Prep: 15m | Ready in: 15m

Ingredients

- 2-1/4 cups crushed chocolate cream-filled sandwich cookies (about 22 cookies)
- 1/3 cup butter, melted
- FILLING:
- 2 packages (8 oz. each) cream cheese, softened
- 1/3 cup confectioners' sugar
- 3 cups vanilla or white chips, melted and cooled
- 1/3 cup heavy whipping cream
- 1 tsp. vanilla extract
- 1/2 cup miniature semisweet chocolate chips
- Additional miniature semisweet chocolate chips, optional

Direction

- Mix butter and cookie crumbs in a small bowl. Push down onto the bottom and up the sides of a greased 9-inch fluted tart pan with a removable bottom. Freeze for at least 1 hour, covered.

- Beat sugar and cream cheese in a large bowl until it turns smooth. Mix in the vanilla, cream and vanilla chips until well blended. Mix in chocolate chips; place over crust. Freeze for 8 hours or overnight, covered.
- Remove the cover and put in the refrigerator for 3-4 hours prior to serving. Sprinkle with miniature chocolate chips if wished. Keep leftovers in the refrigerator.

Nutrition Information
- Calories: 546 calories
- Total Carbohydrate: 53 g
- Cholesterol: 52 mg
- Total Fat: 36 g
- Fiber: 2 g
- Protein: 6 g
- Sodium: 291 mg

Frozen Mocha Cheesecake

"This dessert is a must in a freezer for unanticipated guests."

Serving: 12-16 servings. | Prep: 20m | Ready in: 20m

Ingredients

- CRUST:
- 1-1/2 cups chocolate wafer crumbs
- 2 tbsps. sugar
- 1/3 cup butter, melted
- FILLING:
- 2 packages (8 oz. each) cream cheese, softened
- 1 can (14 oz.) sweetened condensed milk
- 2/3 cup chocolate syrup
- 1 tbsp. instant coffee granules
- 1 tsp. hot water
- 1 cup whipped cream

Direction

- Mix crust ingredients. In a 9-inch springform pan, compress the mixture onto the base of the pan.

- In making the filling, whip cream cheese until smooth in a large bowl. Add syrup and milk gradually. Melt coffee in water; transfer to bowl. Stir in whipped cream by folding. Put into the crust; for at least 6 hours, freeze the cheesecake.

Frozen Mocha Cheesecake Loaf

""A recipe shared by a friend, and it's the exceptional dessert I've ever had. I'm sure that it's packed with calories and fat, though. Can you help?""
Serving: 12 servings. | Prep: 30m | Ready in: 30m

Ingredients

- 2 cups cream-filled chocolate sandwich cookie crumbs
- 3 tbsps. butter, melted
- 1 package (8 oz.) cream cheese, softened
- 1 can (14 oz.) sweetened condensed milk
- 1 tbsp. vanilla extract
- 2 cups heavy whipping cream, whipped
- 2 tbsps. instant coffee granules
- 1 tbsp. hot water
- 1/2 cup chocolate syrup

Direction

- Use heavy-duty foil to line a 9x5-inch loaf pan. Mix butter and cookie crumbs in a small bowl. Then press firmly onto the bottom and 1-1/2inch up the sides of prepare pan. Beat cream cheese in a large bowl until fluffy and light. Mix in vanilla and milk; combine well. Add in whipped cream and fold. Scoop half of the mixture into a separate bowl and reserve. Melt coffee granules in hot water; fold into remaining cream cheese mixture. Mix in chocolate syrup. Scoop half of the chocolate mixture over crust. Put half of the set side cream cheese mixture on top. Repeat layers (pan will be full). Freeze for 6 hours or until set, without cover. Then cover and freeze until serving time. Lift out of pan using foil; cut into slices.

Nutrition Information
- Calories: 423 calories
- Total Carbohydrate: 45 g
- Cholesterol: 67 mg
- Total Fat: 25 g
- Fiber: 2 g
- Protein: 6 g
- Sodium: 268 mg

Frozen Mocha Cheesecakes

""Have fun with various desserts, in this no-bake cheesecake. Make it into a whole new creation by using various flavored chips or mini chips, replacing the coffee with another flavor mix-in or putting in crushed toffee or peppermints. Make sure you put in only 1 tbsp. to avoid overwhelming your taste buds.""
Serving: 8 servings. | Prep: 20m | Ready in: 20m

Ingredients

- 1 egg
- 1/3 cup sugar
- 1/4 cup all-purpose flour
- 2 tbsps. baking cocoa
- 1/4 tsp. vanilla extract
- 3 tbsps. butter, melted
- FILLING:
- 2/3 cup milk chocolate chips
- 4 to 6 tsps. instant coffee granules
- 2 tsps. hot water
- 1 package (8 oz.) cream cheese, softened
- 1 can (14 oz.) sweetened condensed milk
- Whipped cream, optional

Direction

- In a small bowl, combine the first five ingredients; stir in butter. Press onto the bottom of four 4-in.

springform pans coated with cooking spray. Place pans on a baking sheet. Bake at 350° for 12 minutes. Cool on a wire rack. In a microwave, melt chips; stir until smooth Cool. In a small bowl, combine coffee granules and water. In a large bowl, beat the cream cheese, milk, chocolate and coffee mixture until smooth. Pour into crusts. Cover and freeze for at least 6 hours or until firm. Remove from the freezer 15 minutes before serving. Remove sides of pan. Garnish with whipped cream if desired.

Nutrition Information
- Calories: 383 calories
- Total Carbohydrate: 49 g
- Cholesterol: 72 mg
- Total Fat: 18 g
- Fiber: 1 g
- Protein: 9 g
- Sodium: 239 mg

Frozen Mocha Torte

"Each slice of this dessert has a touch of chocolate and mocha. Aside from the fact that it is easy to cook, this delicious recipe looks enchanting and elegant. A must try!"

Serving: 10-12 servings. | Prep: 20m | Ready in: 20m

Ingredients

- 1 cup chocolate wafer crumbs
- 1/4 cup sugar
- 1/4 cup butter, melted
- 1 package (8 oz.) cream cheese, softened
- 1 can (14 oz.) sweetened condensed milk
- 2/3 cup chocolate syrup
- 2 tbsps. instant coffee granules
- 1 tbsp. hot water
- 1 cup heavy whipping cream, whipped
- Chocolate-covered coffee beans, optional

Direction

• Mix butter, wafer crumbs and sugar together in a small bowl. Prepare a 9-inch springform pan by greasing it; add mixture and up the sides 1 inch and on the bottom press it. Let it rest.

• Beat until smooth, the milk, chocolate syrup and cream cheese. In hot water, melt the coffee granules and add it to the cream cheese mixture. Slowly fold in

the whipped cream; pour the mixture into the crust, then cover. Place it in the freezer for about eight hours or overnight.
- Ten to fifteen minutes before dessert time, take it out of the freezer. Loosen from pan by running a knife around the edges. Remove the sides of the pan and decorate your dessert with coffee beans if you like.

Nutrition Information
- Calories: 414 calories
- Total Carbohydrate: 47 g
- Cholesterol: 74 mg
- Total Fat: 23 g
- Fiber: 1 g
- Protein: 6 g
- Sodium: 222 mg

Frozen Raspberry Cheesecake

"This cheesecake recipe was handed down to me by my sister years back and it's easy to make even when you're in a hurry. Perfect for most special occasions because of its elegant look but can be prepare with ingredients readily available. Use different fruits and juices for variation."
Serving: 12 servings. | Prep: 20m | Ready in: 20m

Ingredients

- 1-1/2 cups Oreo cookie crumbs
- 1/4 cup butter, melted
- 1 package (8 oz.) cream cheese, softened
- 3/4 cup confectioners' sugar
- 1 package (10 oz.) frozen sweetened raspberries, thawed
- 3/4 cup cranberry-raspberry juice, divided
- 1 tsp. lemon juice
- 2 cups heavy whipping cream, whipped

Direction

- Mix butter and cookie crumbs and press down onto the bottom of a 9 inches springform pan that's ungreased. Beat confectioner's sugar and cream cheese in a big bowl until smooth. Beat in 1/2 cup cranberry-raspberry juice, raspberries and lemon juice until combined. Fold in whipped cream. Pour onto crust.

• Spoon leftover juice over the cheesecake; use knife to cut through batter and to swirl. Place cover and freeze overnight. Pull out of the freezer 15 minutes prior to serving.

Nutrition Information
• Calories: 319 calories
• Total Carbohydrate: 30 g
• Cholesterol: 58 mg
• Total Fat: 22 g
• Fiber: 2 g
• Protein: 3 g
• Sodium: 186 mg

Fudge Truffle Cheesecake

""The cheesecake is a truffle-like chocolate over a chocolate cookie bottom. Ditch your partner if it doesn't make them crazy. Note: Toppings can be customized from chocolate dipped strawberries, commercial chocolate truffles, melted white or dark chocolate and drizzle on top whichever fits your liking.""

Serving: 14 | Prep: 30m | Ready in: 5h

Ingredients

- 1 1/2 cups vanilla wafer crumbs
- 1/2 cup confectioners' sugar
- 1/3 cup unsweetened cocoa powder
- 1/3 cup butter, softened
- 2 cups semi-sweet chocolate chips
- 3 (8 oz.) packages cream cheese, room temperature
- 1 (14 oz.) can sweetened condensed milk
- 4 eggs
- 2 tsps. vanilla extract

Direction

- Preheat the oven to temperature of 150°C or 300°F.

- Manually combine crushed vanilla wafers, cocoa, confectioners' sugar and butter in a big mixing bowl. Flatten the crust into a 9-inch sized springform pan.

- Melt chocolate chips over double boiler until smooth. Using an electric mixer, beat the cream cheese until fluffy and slowly add condensed milk until it's smooth. Then add the melted chocolate, vanilla and eggs under low speed until all ingredients are completely mixed. Pour the mixture over crust.
- Bake for 55 minutes at 300 °F or 150°C. It is fine if the cake seems under-baked in the middle as it continues to bake when taken out of the oven.
- Cool to room temperature and place in refrigerator for some time before eating.

Nutrition Information
- Calories: 552 calories;
- Total Carbohydrate: 51.4 g
- Cholesterol: 127 mg
- Total Fat: 35.9 g
- Protein: 10.6 g
- Sodium: 288 mg

German Chocolate Cake Cheesecake

""This yummy and rich dessert is my cheesecake version of German chocolate cake. It creates a classic to a special meal.""

Serving: 12 servings. | Prep: 30m | Ready in: 01h20m

Ingredients

- 1-1/2 cups chocolate graham cracker crumbs (about 8 whole crackers)
- 2 tbsps. brown sugar
- 1/4 cup butter, melted
- FILLING:
- 2 packages (8 oz. each) cream cheese, softened
- 1 cup (6 oz.) semisweet chocolate chips, melted and cooled
- 2/3 cup packed brown sugar
- 2 tbsps. baking cocoa
- 5 eggs, lightly beaten
- 1 tsp. almond extract
- 1 tsp. vanilla extract
- TOPPING:
- 3/4 cup sweetened shredded coconut
- 3/4 cup chopped walnuts
- 1/3 cup packed brown sugar
- 1/3 cup half-and-half cream
- 5 tbsps. butter

Direction

- On a double thickness of heavy-duty foil (about 18in. square), put a greased 9-inch springform pan. Tightly wrap foil around the pan. Mix in a small bowl the brown sugar and cracker crumbs; mix in butter.
- Then press onto the bottom and 1-inch up the sides of the prepared pan. Move the pan to a baking sheet. Place in the oven and bake for 10 minutes at 350°F. Put on a wire rack and cool.
- Beat cream cheese in a large bowl until it turns smooth. Mix in the cocoa, brown sugar and chocolate. Put in eggs; whisk on low speed just until combined. Mix in extracts. Then put into the crust.
- Put the pan in a large baking pan. Fill with 1-inch water into the larger pan. Place in the oven and bake for 50-55 minutes at 350°F or until middle is just set and top looks dull. Take out springform pan from water bath. Put on a wire rack and cool for 10 minutes. Cautiously run a knife around the edge of a pan to loosen; cool for 1 more hour. Keep in the refrigerator for 4 hours or overnight. Take off sides of the pan.
- Mix in a large saucepan the topping ingredients. Make it boil over medium heat; stir and cook for 3 minutes. Let it cool. Place the topping over the cheesecake and spread. Keep leftovers in the refrigerator.

Nutrition Information
- Calories: 449 calories
- Total Carbohydrate: 42 g

- Cholesterol: 136 mg
- Total Fat: 30 g
- Fiber: 2 g
- Protein: 8 g
- Sodium: 257 mg

German Chocolate Cheesecake Squares

""I have a hard time choosing my all-time well-love recipe when everyone ask me about. But this one is surely tops among sweet.""

Serving: 3 dozen. | Prep: 50m | Ready in: 01h10m

Ingredients

- 1 package (1/4 oz.) active dry yeast
- 1/2 cup warm water (110° to 115°)
- 1/4 cup sugar
- 1/2 tsp. salt
- 1 large egg
- 1/2 cup butter, softened
- 2 to 2-1/2 cups all-purpose flour
- FILLING:
- 2 packages (8 oz. each) cream cheese, softened
- 1/3 cup baking cocoa
- 1 cup sugar
- 3 large eggs
- 2 tsps. vanilla extract
- TOPPING:
- 1/2 cup sugar
- 1 large egg
- 1/2 cup evaporated milk
- 1/4 cup butter
- 1 tsp. vanilla extract
- 2/3 cup sweetened shredded coconut
- 1/2 cup chopped pecans

Direction

- Melt yeast in water in a large bowl. Put in 1 cup of flour, butter, egg, salt and sugar; mix until smooth. Put in enough remaining flour to make a soft dough. Then place onto a floured surface; massage for about 3-5 minutes until elastic and smooth. Put in greased bowl, flipping once to grease top. Allow to rest, covered, for 20 minutes. Smash dough down. Then press onto the bottom and up the sides of a greased 15x10x1-inch baking pan. Whip cream cheese in a large bowl until smooth; gently add sugar and cocoa. Whisk until turns fluffy. Mix in eggs, one at a time. Put in vanilla. Place into crust. Place in the oven and bake for 20-25 minutes at 350°F or until crust is golden brown; then cool. Mix in a saucepan the first four topping ingredients; cook for about 8-10 minutes over low heat until thick, whisking constantly. Separate from heat; mix in nuts, coconut and vanilla. Spread over cooled caked. Let chill for at least 1 hour. Keep in the refrigerator.

Nutrition Information
- Calories: 157 calories
- Total Carbohydrate: 17 g
- Cholesterol: 48 mg
- Total Fat: 9 g
- Fiber: 1 g
- Protein: 3 g
- Sodium: 107 mg

www.ingramcontent.com/pod-product-compliance
Lightning Source LLC
Chambersburg PA
CBHW071439070526
44578CB00001B/146